People's Guide:
Dog Care

Series Editor • Jason Flynn

BORDERS.

Published by
Adams Media, an F+W Publications Company
57 Littlefield Street, Avon, MA 02322
www.adamsmedia.com

ISBN: 1-59337-612-X
Contains portions of material adapted and abridged from *The Everything® Dog Book*
by Carlo DeVito with Amy Ammen, ©1990, F+W Publications. Additonal material
provided by Sue Owens Wright.

Printed in Canada.
J   I   H   G   F   E   D   C   B   A

Library of Congress Cataloging-in-Publication Data
Flynn, Jason.
Dog care / Jason Flynn.
p. cm. -- (People's guide)
ISBN 1-59337-612-X
1. Dogs. I. Title. II. Series.
SF427.F59 2005
636.7--dc22

2005020252

This publication is designed to provide accurate and authoritative information with
regard to the subject matter covered. It is sold with the understanding that the
publisher is not engaged in rendering legal, accounting, or other professional advice.
If legal advice or other expert assistance is required, the services of a competent
professional person should be sought.

—From a *Declaration of Principles* jointly adopted
by a Committee of the American Bar Association and a
Committee of Publishers and Associations

Many of the designations used by manufacturers and sellers to distinguish their
products are claimed as trademarks. Where those designations appear in this book
and Adams Media was aware of a trademark claim, the designations have been
printed with initial capital letters.

For bulk sales, contact your local Borders store and ask to speak to the Corporate
Sales Representative.

Table of Contents

Introduction

If you have this book in your hands, odds are very good you love dogs already. It could be because of a childhood pet that you adored, a neighbor's dog that you always wanted to play with or just the joy of watching someone play with a loveable pup and wanting to have that for yourself.

Unfortunately, taking care of a dog is more work than you might imagine. There's nutrition, grooming, health care, and other responsibilities that you might not have even considered. But you are ahead of the game. In picking up *People's Guide: Dog Care*, you'll find a wide variety of information to help you with everything from choosing the type of dog you want, figuring out what to feed your new friend, and loads of solid practical health-care advice that will aid you in becoming a responsible owner.

PART 1

CHOOSING A DOG

CHAPTER 1

Why to Get a Dog and Other Questions to Ask

There is nothing better than coming home from a hard day's work to a tail-wagging, sloppy-tongued mop of a dog who can't wait to greet you. Dogs are bouncy and loving and wonderful—there's no getting around it, they're wonderful companions. They are fun, friendly, and love attention. They love to play, go for long walks, and be mischievous.

But know going in that dogs are a tremendous amount of responsibility. It's fun to cuddle up with a dog while watching television, or take him hiking and running; it's fun to play with a dog at the beach, in a park, or in the snow. But dogs also require forethought and attention, even on days when we would rather think only of ourselves.

Every year, thousands of dogs are left homeless and are sheltered in dog pounds and rescue homes all across the country.

Often this is no fault of the dog's. When the cute puppy turns eight months old and starts showing an ornery streak, that can be the last straw. When an over-obliging owner suddenly finds himself with a dog who growls when he's told to get off the bed, well, the dog may become a casualty. People give up their dogs because they didn't fully understand doggy behavior and all the things that need to be done to keep a dog healthy and well-behaved. They find out that dalmatians require too much exercise; they didn't know Saint Bernards grew *that* big!; those tiny Maltese are mischievous balls of fire. Suddenly Rover finds himself at the shelter with a haunted look on his face, cowering at the back of his pen, as countless strangers pass by and he remains alone. In an era when so much of our world is about immediate gratification and making almost anything disposable, dogs are no exceptions. Unfortunately, they pay for being disposable with their lives. In fact, every year, thousands of dogs are put down because of neglect or homelessness.

A big reason this happens is that many people don't think before they add a dog to their lives. Don't let this happen to you! Ask yourself some important questions before you go running out to get the dog your kids are screaming for or that you think will fill the gap in your life: What kind of life do you lead? How much room do you have, and what kind of house do you live in? What kind of attention do you think you can offer the animal? Will someone be home all day to housetrain and socialize a puppy? Do you have a fenced yard? How old are your children? Does everyone in the family want a dog, or are you caving in to one demanding child? Do you want an active dog, a laid-back dog, a big dog, a small dog, a hairy dog, a hairless dog, a slobbery dog, a neat dog? With more than 140 American Kennel Club recognized breeds to choose from, and plenty of mixed breeds, you can really pinpoint the kind of dog that will suit your lifestyle.

So take this time to think about what you and your family want. Be responsible, and enjoy the comfort, love, and happiness that owning a dog can bring for a long time to come.

WHAT KIND OF DOG WILL FIT INTO MY LIFESTYLE?

We're not talking about *Martha Stewart* or *Better Homes & Gardens* style. You can't pick out a dog because you think he'll look good with your sofa, or he'll go well with your English garden. You don't pick out a dog that matches your Ralph Lauren outfit or goes with your rugged Levis and Timberlands. This is not how you pick your dog. A dog is not a designer emblem. It's an animal with a mind of its own and a sense of humor all its own. It's like having another person in the house!

What is your idea of fun? Rollerblading? Riding your bike? Watching a movie or sports on television? Going hiking? Going on little day trips in the car? Going to the park or beach and lying out in the sun? Do you work? Part-time? Full-time? Are you one of those career sociopaths who puts in seventy hours a week? Do you like to come home, shower, and go back out to dinner and the movies or your favorite bar? Are you obsessively neat? Are you allergic to pets? You have to ask yourself these kinds of questions when you are choosing a dog so that you can pick the dog that's best for you.

It's important to think about your life before you buy your dog, so that six months later poor Fido isn't back out on the street looking for a new job. You don't want to be coming home and cursing your happy little pooch, just because he's at home drawing breath, keeping you from meeting your soulmate at tonight's hottest party.

Many times people who don't think about what kind of dog they really want are at cross purposes with their dog. You don't want a pet that's going to cramp your style. And of course, you don't want to pick a dog whose life you're going to make miserable.

If you're an in-line skater, you want to know that when you come home, you can suit up, put a leash on Rover, and bring him along. You want a dog who shares in that fun. You need an athletic dog who has the stamina and explosive energy to keep up with you. You don't want some sedentary hound who's panting after the first half-mile. Likewise, if you like going for an evening stroll, you don't want some drooling half-lunatic pulling you around the block like a crazed demon. You want a good dog who shares your pace and enjoyment of the evening air.

Maybe you need a dog who can keep up with your children and whom you can trust to watch over them. You need your dog to be, not a substitute parent or some kind of living, unbreakable toy, but a companion and playmate for your kids to share in their well-behaved fun.

VISIT A SHOW ROOM . . .

The best way to find out about the idiosyncrasies of various breeds, and to really get a good look at them, is to go to dog shows. You'll find representatives of just about all the American Kennel Club breeds at a dog show, and best of all, you'll find their breeders, the people who understand them best. Not only that, because you'll get to look around and talk to so many people, you may leave with a completely different idea about what kind of dog you want than you had before you went to the show.

For example, you may think a beagle will suit everyone in your family fine. He'll be small enough for the kids, solid enough to be played with, active enough to go on family outings, and not so big you feel he'll take over your small house. When you go to the dog show intent on meeting some local breeders and finding out if they have puppies available, you may see the beagles in the ring and decide that something about them doesn't appeal to you at all. They always have their noses to the ground; they bark at other dogs too often; they seem aloof. And just as you feel your heart sink, your son tugs your sleeve and says, "Look, what's that?" and you fall in love with a West Highland white terrier.

Seeing is believing, and being able to talk to breeders is invaluable. Breeders are used to dealing with people in the same situation as you. Also, they are concerned that the dogs they breed find the right homes for them. A Husky breeder would not recommend that one of her pups go to a home in which the primary caretaker was wheelchair-bound. That wouldn't be fair to the person, and it wouldn't be fair to the dog.

How do you find dog shows to attend? Call the veterinary offices in or near your town. They should know the names of breeders who can tell you if shows are coming up in the area. You can call the American Kennel Club and ask for show information. The AKC's customer service number is (919) 233-9767. You can also find show information on the AKC's Web page, www.akc.org.

TALKING TO BREEDERS

As mentioned earlier, breeders are your best source of information about a dog you are interested in. After all, these folks are passionate about their breed! They've lived with it, some for several decades, and can tell you the breed's positive and negative qualities.

Breeders will interview you, too, which will help you decide if the breed is truly right for you. A breeder may ask you how often you like to go hiking, say, or how often you travel. You may realize you're not the sportsperson you thought you were, or that your schedule is tighter than you thought. Then again, you may be relieved to hear that a breed you thought was too active actually doesn't need as much exercise as you thought, and the breeder has helped you figure out how to fit in a good workout for the dog without compromising your daily habits.

Another great thing about talking to breeders is that you will get a good sense of who you want to get your puppy (or older dog) from. The person who's especially helpful, or with whom you "click," or whose dogs seem the most well-behaved and mellow of the lot you've spoken with—this is the person from whom you want to acquire your new family member. You should feel comfortable calling your breeder at any time during your dog's life to ask him or her about any kind of problems you're having. If your pup's chewing is getting out of control, or if housetraining isn't working, or if your adult dog suddenly goes lame, it's nice to know there's someone you can call who not only knows the breed, but knows your dog personally.

A responsible breeder will tell you all about your potential puppy's or older dog's past—what the parents and siblings are like, whether there's working stock in the bloodlines, what kind of traits he's been breeding away from (or for), particular health problems to look out for, and much more. In fact, a breeder who doesn't want to inform you of all these things, particularly health records for breeds prone to hip dysplasia or other genetic conditions, is one to stay away from—he's probably got something to hide.

Responsible breeders want their puppies or older dogs to find homes in which they'll be loved and cared for as real family members for the duration of their lives. Many of them will put in writing that if for any reason you can't keep the dog any longer, you'll contact them first before surrendering the dog to a shelter. Doesn't this sound like the kind of grandma or grandpa you want for your dog?

DOCTOR, DOCTOR

Studies prove that veterinarians are the first ones most pet owners turn to for help with a variety of problems, from health to behavior. And because they're on the "front lines" of dealing with various breeds and their owners, they can give you some solid advice about general traits of some breeds.

The veterinarians at the clinic nearest you may know that Labrador retrievers are being overbred in the area, and they're seeing a lot of chewing, digging, and nervous behavior problems. They may be able to tell you that 70 percent of all German shepherds they see develop hip dysplasia. They may also tell you that bichon frisés make ideal family pets. It's important to remember that even though they see a lot of different dogs, they are not experts on all breeds.

What is important is that once you've chosen your puppy or dog, you need to establish a relationship with a veterinarian you can trust completely. If a veterinarian makes you feel silly about asking a basic question, or doesn't seem to want to spend much time examining your animal, keep shopping until you find someone you can discuss anything with. It's the same scenario as shopping for a breeder—this is someone you'll trust your dog's life with.

A LITTLE FRIENDLY ADVICE

Now, you may be fortunate enough to have friends who are long time dog people. Responsible and knowledge dog owners who can help you tremendously in your search. They can pass along the

names of breeders, vets, and shelters they know and trust, not to
mention providing a steady and trustworthy source of information.

If you don't have dog people in your circle of friends, you
should strike up a conversation with friends and loved ones before
you make up your mind about bringing a dog into your life. Why?
Your friends can offer you an honest assessment of your habits,
hobbies, and lifestyle that you might not have considered. Are you
fooling yourself into thinking that you can afford to have a large-
sized dog in your tiny apartment? A friend will be much more
likely to give you a blunt reminder you need.

PUREBRED OR MIXED BREED?

There is a lot of information written about purebreds because
they've been selectively bred to look and act in particular ways. This
should make choosing a dog to join your family simpler. But it can
also make it seem quite complicated! There are so many choices; so
much to do; so many things to think about. After investigating all
the breeds, you may find that none especially does it for you.

If you're worn out on the purebred route, or it simply doesn't
matter that much to you how much you know about your dog's genetic makeup, you may want to adopt a mixed-breed dog. Yes, a
mutt! These may not be the most beautiful dogs you've ever seen,
and you may never be sure whether their instincts are coming from
retriever blood or terrier blood or perhaps a bit of everything—but
like their purebred cousins, mixed breeds can make superlative pets.

Mixed-breed dogs often marry the best traits of the dogs
they're descended from. It is fun to try to guess what breeds went
into making your dog. In some cases you'll know—if your Lab
bred the Australian cattle dog next door by mistake—but in many
cases you won't know at all.

In the end, neither a purebred or a mixed breed is going to be a better dog than the other. Both are just dogs. The important considerations are, again, how well your lifestyle accommodates your dog's basic needs. If he's a big hairy purebred or a big hairy mix and you're a neat freak who lives in a fifth-floor walkup, things might not work out. Whether you choose purebred or mixed, you have to realistically assess the amount of time and energy you have to take care of your dog the way he deserves (and needs) to be taken care of. Remember, while quality breeding is important to keep the various breeds alive, dogs, unlike humans, don't differentiate between breed and nonbreed. Dogs only care that you are their primary caregiver and leader. It's only people who differentiate between purebred and mutt.

PUPPY OR ADULT?

This is a question most people don't stop to think about, but should. Most of the time when people think of getting a dog, they think about getting a puppy. They think of the cute ball of fluff running around the house making the family laugh. They want to nurture and raise the dog from a pup.

Do You Really Want a Puppy?

Think about it: Do you really want a puppy? Is a puppy the best fit with your family's lifestyle? Having a puppy is like having a two-year-old in the house. Puppies want to get into everything, and they use their mouths to explore. They need to chew, and if you don't supply a variety of toys, they'll chew what's available. Puppies need to be kept on very strict schedules in order to be housetrained. That means taking the puppy out first thing in the morning, several times during the day, and last thing at night. It means monitoring the puppy during the day to try to prevent accidents from

happening. It means making a real commitment to training and socializing, because when your puppy gets big and he doesn't know
what's expected of him, he'll make the rules. It may be cute to have
your puppy curl up on the couch with you or sleep in your bed or
jump up on you to greet you, but then don't be surprised if you meet
with resistance when your pup's grown up and you don't want him
doing those things anymore.

What Older Dogs Have to Offer

When you get an older dog, you obviously miss those early days
of playfulness and cuteness. But you do get other things in return.
Older dogs are generally calmer; they're usually housetrained; they're
more set in their ways; and people report that they seem grateful to
be in a new home in which they're loved and appreciated.

There's also the feel-good part of getting an older dog, because whether you adopt one from a shelter or a purebred rescue
group or just take one in from a neighbor, you are essentially sav-
ing that dog's life. Yes, you are inheriting behaviors that the dog
has learned from its previous owners or circumstances, but con-
trary to the old saying, you can teach an old dog new tricks. And if
you approach getting an older dog as conscientiously as you would
approach getting a puppy, you're sure to find one whose temperament suits you, for better or worse.

Adopting an older dog doesn't mean going to the dog pound
and rescuing a mangy mutt on death row (though those who do
are blessed). There are many older dogs available, both purebred
(through breed-supported rescue groups as well as the local shelters) and mixed-breed, that are physically and mentally sound. The
obvious thing about taking in an older dog is that you're making a
difference in a dog's life. But the thing you need to consider is: Is
an adult dog going to make a difference in your life?

CHAPTER 2

Dog Organizations and What They Offer

MEMBERSHIP HAS ITS BENEFITS

In today's world, for every kind of lifestyle people lead, there is a different kind of dog. There are tiny dogs and giant dogs, hairless and shaggy, pedigreed and mutt. And there are many organizations out there that are very helpful in understanding what dogs are all about and are willing to help you.

Different clubs have different aims, but they all share several things in common. First, they are very much into promoting dogs, and shining the best possible light on the breeds they favor or the agenda they promote. Second, they are indeed intended to help people understand dogs better. Although many of the most popular organizations have political reasons for agreeing or disagreeing with each other, the one thing they certainly share is their love of our canine friends.

Many of these clubs offer many pamphlets on choosing a dog, training, spaying, pet health care, and many other things that go along with responsible pet ownership. They offer many valuable tools, some of which are free, to make you a good fit with your dog. They are also doing everything they can to encourage pet owners to be more considerate of their non-pet-owning neighbors. No one wants to live near a dog that doesn't mind its master—who runs around jumping up on people and bothering them. While you might think your "puppy" is the best, cutest, cuddliest, friendliest little animal ever to grace the face of the earth, there is always someone out there who sees your dog for the slobbering, dirty, ill-mannered beast he or she really is. Good manners go a long way, especially in close-knit communities.

All of these different kinds of organizations are broken up into two categories: breed registries and animal advocacy groups. Breed registries are more concerned with breed standards and quality, while animal advocacy groups are aimed more at the prevention of cruelty and sheltering strays.

THE AMERICAN KENNEL CLUB

The most famous organization that represents purebred dogs in the United States (and arguably the world) is the American Kennel Club. Established in 1884 to advance the interests of purebred dogs, today the American Kennel Club recognizes more than 140 breeds in seven groups (Sporting, Non-Sporting, Working, Herding, Terrier, Hound, and Toy). It is a nonprofit organization whose members are not individual dog owners, but breed clubs. Each member club (and there are currently about 500 of them) elects a delegate to represent the club at AKC meetings. The delegates vote on the rules of the sport of dogs—they are the legislative body of the American Kennel Club. The delegates elect the AKC's twelve-member Board of Directors, who are responsible for the overall and daily management of the organization.

Most people are familiar with the prestigious Westminster Kennel Club show that's televised from Madison Square Garden every February. Westminster is one of the member clubs of the AKC—one of the oldest, too. Besides the hundreds of member clubs, there are nearly 5,000 affiliated clubs that conduct AKC events (dog shows and other events) following AKC rules of conduct. Believe it or not, purebred dog fanciers participate in more than 3,000 dog shows a year, as well as more than 5,000 performance events.

The AKC oversees the establishment of recognized breeds in the United States, and also enforces the standards by which breeds are judged. To carry out its many functions, the AKC maintains offices in New York City (where it was founded) and Raleigh, North Carolina. It has several divisions: Registration, of course, but also Judges' Education, Performance Events, Publications, and more. The AKC maintains a reference library of more than 15,000 books, including editions of some of the earliest books ever published on dogs.

What does all this mean to you? It means that when you buy a purebred puppy and register it, you are joining a very large and time-honored family of people who are crazy about dogs. If you want, you can look up fifty generations of your golden retriever's ancestors. That's what being purebred means—not that your puppy is some kind of elite dog, but rather, that all the caretakers of his family before you wanted to breed the same kind of dog over and over. The AKC's purpose is to preserve the integrity of its registry of purebred dogs, to sanction events that promote the purpose and function of purebred dogs, and to ultimately protect and ensure the continuation of the sport. The AKC works very hard to make sure that the dogs it registers and awards show points, championships, and performance titles to are the best examples of their breed. However, the AKC is quick to point out that having an "AKC registered dog" does not necessarily mean your dog will be free of health problems, or that it is of championship quality. All it means is that your dog's parents are registered purebreds, and that those dogs' parents are registered purebreds, and so on.

OTHER BREED REGISTRIES IN THE UNITED STATES

The AKC is not the only registry organization in the United States or the world. There are many others, with varying philosophies and programs.

The United Kennel Club

The United Kennel Club was founded in 1898 by Chauncey Z. Bennett. The UKC registers more than a quarter-million dogs each year. Their largest number of registrations are for American Pit Bull Terriers. Those two important facts make the UKC the second oldest and second largest all-breed dog registry in the United States. They are located in Kalamazoo, Michigan.

The UKC, like the AKC, sponsors events of many kinds, from dog shows to a host of performance events. The UKC is made up of 1,200 different clubs that oversee 10,000 licensed annual dog events. Many of their events are very easy to enter and compete in, promoting owners to show and compete with their dogs, as opposed to hiring professional trainers or handlers.

UKC offers something called the P.A.D. (Pups And Degrees) performance pedigree. This is basically a tracking system which records all the puppies a registered dog has produced and follows those puppies and their performance in the ring. The UKC also sponsors a program for DNA profiling of your puppy, in association with PE Zoogen, a DNA testing firm.

Lesser-Known Registries

The AKC and the UKC only recognize 144 and 188 breeds, respectively. And, believe it or not, there are people out there buying dogs that don't have established dog clubs and organizations behind them. These people find it very hard to compete for pure-breed championships. For example, neither the AKC nor the UKC register the Dogo Argentino. Sometimes, smaller clubs fill these voids. The American Rare Breed Association (ARBA) and the American Mixed Breed Obedience Registry (AMBOR) allow members to join with their dogs and compete in various sponsored events.

The Canadian Kennel Club

Much like the AKC, the CKC is the primary registering and overseer organization of the sport of purebred dogs in Canada. Many Canadians who want to compete in the United States register their dogs in both clubs. Much like the AKC, the Canadian Kennel Club is devoted to encouraging, guiding, and advancing the interests of purebred dogs and their owners and breeders in Canada.

PET ADVOCACY GROUPS

The American Society for the Prevention of Cruelty to Animals

The American Society for the Prevention of Cruelty to Animals is one of the most active pro-pet groups in the world. A nonprofit company, the ASPCA sponsors countless numbers of groups and events to protect animals' and pet owners' rights. The ASPCA has attempted to reduce pain, fear, and suffering in animals through humane law enforcement, legislative advocacy, education, and hands-on animal care.

The ASPCA was founded in 1866 by a diplomat named Henry Bergh, who served in the U.S. delegation to Russia. Bergh modeled the ASPCA on England's Royal SPCA. The ASPCA managed to get the nation's first anti-cruelty laws passed in the state of New York in its first year. The ASPCA provided ambulance service to horses in New York City two years before the first hospital provided them for humans. In seven short years, twenty-five states, a number of territories, and Canada had used the ASPCA as a model for their own humane organizations.

Today, the ASPCA supplies a number of different services to pet and animal lovers all across the country. They are perhaps best known for helping shelter strays and foster adoptions. Their foster care program encourages sympathetic homes to help animals who are "too young, sick or aggressive to be offered for adoption right away a chance to have a long and healthy life by placing them in temporary homes."

People often confuse the New York-based ASPCA with other SPCAs around the country. There are Societies for the Prevention of Cruelty to Animals (SPCAs) in many states.

The Humane Society of the United States

The Humane Society of the United States (HSUS) is another of the nation's largest animal-protection organizations. While the ASPCA is more focused on pets, especially dogs and cats, the Humane Society has a much wider scope. HSUS promotes the "humane treatment of animals and to foster respect, understanding, and compassion for all creatures." The HSUS uses such venues as the legal system, education, and legislation to ensure the protection of animals of all kinds.

The HSUS was founded in 1954 and currently has nine major offices in the United States. Unlike the ASPCA, the HSUS does not have any affiliate shelters. The HSUS mainly concerns itself with wildlife protection, companion animals, and animal research violations. However, they do sponsor many events for pet owners and do encourage pet rescue (adoption). Some of the events they sponsor include free spaying clinics for pet owners of insufficient means.

The American Humane Association

Founded in 1877, the American Humane Association (AHA) is a welfare organization involved in assisting both animals and children. These days the AHA oversees the treatment of animals on movie and television sets and is working to establish standards for dog trainers, among many other things.

CHAPTER 3

Where to Get Your Dog

BREEDERS

Certainly, you would think, this is like asking a Chevrolet sales-man if he himself would buy a Chevrolet. What do you think he's going to tell you? "Oh, no, I think you're much more a Honda type. Honda's down the road." But if you get a good breeder, he or she may indeed tell you just that.

Not enough breeders are that responsible. There are plenty of breeders who don't ask the tough questions. There are many who don't have any scruples at all. That's why it's important to find a reputable breeder whom you can trust.

PET SHOPS

Are the dogs you can buy in a pet shop any different than the ones you can buy from a breeder? More times than not, absolutely. As we've discussed, a responsible breeder insures that his or her dogs

are bred for a purpose, that they're properly raised and social-
ized, and that any health problems have been addressed. He or she
takes care to breed two dogs who complement each other in order
to produce the best possible dog, most emblematic of the breed
standard or ideal. Responsible breeders ask you a lot of questions
before they agree to sell you a puppy, and they try to match your
personality with one of their puppies.

Many pet shops get their dogs from breeders the media have
labeled "puppy mills." These breeders produce dogs with little or
no concern about breed standards, temperament, or health problems. As a result, unsuspecting buyers don't know what they're
getting. These dogs are as purebred as the dogs you get from a
breeder, because purebred only means the mother and father are
registered purebreds. These puppies are also as cute as the ones
you'll see at a responsible breeder's, though they may lack the energy or robust appearance of the responsible breeder's pups.

Pet shops know that puppies are most appealing when they're
six to eight weeks old. That means that to get them to the store
by that age they are usually separated from their mother and littermates at four to six weeks of age—far too early. These pups
miss the nutritional and behavioral benefits of staying in their first
family for as long as they should, and their new families pay the
price in health and behavior problems later in life.

Does this mean good dogs don't come from pet shops? Pet
shops are under a lot of pressure from the general public to sell
them healthy puppies. More and more, they either don't sell puppies or they host adoption days where local shelters come in so
people can get their dogs from the shelter. This is good PR for the
pet shop and good business for the shelter. It also makes people
feel better about the dog they're acquiring.

If you do buy a puppy from a pet store, ask the staff a lot of questions about its background and whether the store provides any guarantees of the puppy's health. Take the puppy to a veterinarian right away for a first physical, and if the vet suspects any problems, speak with the store staff immediately.

PUREBRED RESCUE

A "rescue" dog is a purebred dog who has been "rescued" from a former home or from a pound or shelter and is currently homeless. Most AKC breed clubs sponsor purebred rescue groups. When a dog is dropped off at the shelter or taken into the dog pound, if that dog is believed to be purebred, that local shelter calls the contact person for the local rescue group. If the rescue coordinator believes the dog is a purebred of the breed with which he or she is involved, that dog is taken from the pound and housed in a foster home until the rescue organization can find the dog a home.

Rescue is run generally by breeders who are very concerned about dogs in general. They make no money off this and usually work on a volunteer basis. Much of the cost of fostering is picked up by the family that is sheltering the dog in their house. Each breed has a specific network of these people who have extremely big hearts and only want to see the dogs find a good home.

Do these dogs have something wrong with them? Generally speaking, no. They have been housed by people who could no longer properly care for their animals. Sometimes this is brought about by a death in the family or by difficult circumstances. Rescue coordinators bail out abandoned or unwanted dogs and evaluate them before seeking new homes for them. Many rescue dogs need some stability to help regain their confidence, and foster owners spend a lot of time working with such animals to ensure that they'll adjust to a new home.

They then list the dog with a national or regional network, where the dog will eventually be placed. Generally speaking, all kinds of dogs pass through this scenario. They tend to be a little older than puppies. They can be anywhere from 18 months to 10 years old. They come in all shapes, sizes, and temperaments. The only thing they have in common is that they are all purebreds.

Because they are rescue dogs, they also tend to be cheaper than their puppy counterparts. The rescue associations usually ask you to make some kind of donation to defray the costs of operating the rescue group and the costs of the individual dog. These groups are run by loving individuals who are looking earnestly for the right home for the right dog. You should seriously consider this venue as a means to getting a dog.

SHELTERS/POUNDS

Many local animal shelters are in operation all over the United States. Some dogs are brought there by their current owners, or by the families of those persons. Sometimes the dogs are found on the side of the road and are brought in by a concerned citizen who can't shelter the animal, or they are brought in by the local animal control department.

Many times these dogs are perfectly fine animals who just need a home. In many cases, the animals take a little time to adjust when you first bring them home. Dogs want to be part of a pack. Being moved from pack to pack undermines a dog's self-assurance. As pack position is very important to how a dog sees him or herself, being separated and then situated into a new pack definitely plays games with poor Rover's head. The longer a dog stays with you, the more secure it will become in its surroundings and the more comfortable it will feel with you.

Sometimes the shelters have lots of information on a particular dog, and sometimes they have none. But many of the people who work in shelters are there because they love animals and spend great amounts of time with them. They are often the best judges of how these dogs are and what they like and don't like. They can tell you how they respond to certain things and to other dogs.

In short, if you don't care about purebred vs. mixed breed, there are plenty of dogs that need good homes in these shelters. When you bring them home, they need a little extra loving and space before they can become confident, but they'll make it up to you with love and admiration. In many cases, they're a little older and are already housetrained. Later on, we'll talk about the special needs of rescue and shelter dogs when you first bring them home.

FRIENDS

This is probably one of the least likely—and least desirable—places to get a dog. How much does your friend know about breeding dogs? Maybe he has great fashion sense, knows all the newest, hottest bands, hangs out with cool people, has a great job—but what does he really know about dogs?

Often people have puppies to give away because their dog got pregnant. Sometimes they've bred her to another dog, and sometimes she's found a beau of her own. Although dogs may think they're picky, however, you should know that they don't differentiate by breed. They either like another dog, or they don't.

In many cases, you really don't know what you're getting. And that's when you have to ask yourself a lot of questions. Is my friend really good to his or her dog? Did they read up on what to do with a pregnant dog? Did they go to their veterinarian and get his or her advice? Do I like my friend's dog? Have I spent enough time with that dog to know whether or not I like it?

PART 2

BASIC DOG CARE

CHAPTER 4

Getting Your Home and Your Dog Ready

Bringing Your New Puppy or Dog Home

You've actually picked a dog and the arrival date is near. Now comes one of the most important parts: preparing for your newest little bundle of joy. This is a tougher job than you'd imagine. But it's also fun. The excitement of bringing home your new puppy is wonderful, but don't let some safety precautions elude you in the midst of all the excitement. First, take a look around your home. What do you need to do so that Puppy doesn't destroy all your family's prized possessions, and so he doesn't hurt himself chewing on something that could be harmful? Where will Puppy sleep? What will he eat, and out of what? How will you take him outside? These are the considerations that affect what kind of "equipment" and other supplies you'll need to make sure you and your dog get off to a good start.

The one thing to remember is that whether you're bringing home a new puppy or an older dog, there are still things you'll want to do to protect your house and your dog from any possible disasters.

PUPPY-PROOFING YOUR HOME

Phase 1

The first thing you want to do with a puppy is limit the amount of space in which he can run around—especially when you're not home. Many people confine the pup to a room or group of manageable rooms in the beginning. Choose a room in which there's a lot of people traffic so your puppy doesn't feel isolated. Pick a room that's fairly easy to clean up, with an easily washable floor surface. Pick a room that's light and airy. The kitchen or washroom are good first choices, whether you're crate-training your puppy or not (and you should be; more on that later!).

There's no way around it—if you're getting a puppy, and you want to limit his space, you need a baby gate. He will not be in his crate all the time, yet he might not be trustworthy enough in his housetraining to have free run of other rooms. Baby gates do a good job of setting up a solid barrier while allowing the puppy to see into the other room and also smell what's going on in there (very important to a dog). Another nice thing about baby gates is that they're portable and removable. Once Puppy's good in the kitchen and the den, for example, you can put a gate up in front of the stairs or in doorways leading to rooms that are still off limits. Buy the baby gate(s) and save yourself a lot of time and aggravation.

Why do you want to confine your puppy (or new dog)? It's for his benefit and yours. When you're not home, it limits the amount of damage he can do to himself or the house to just one room. Before you leave, if you're not going to be crating Junior, it's easier for you to look around and either move or hide away things that might cause him harm.

Once you've put the baby gates up, you need to look around the room and ask yourself the following question: If you were a dog, what would you chew on? The usual answer: everything. If there are exposed wires, cover them up. The chairs around the kitchen table? If they're wood, put them in the attic for now. Are all bottles and cans out of the way? Are all cleansers and other potentially toxic substances safe inside child-proof cabinets? And don't forget: Hide the garbage. Garbage is the dinner of the gourmet dog. Everything wonderful and edible is in the garbage and your puppy knows it. Move it, or come home every day and wonder what condition your house and your dog are going to be in. What can't be moved, especially anything that's made out of wood, spray with a product called bitter apple. Bitter apple usually comes in a spray. It leaves a very bitter taste on things that deters dogs from chewing.

However, you must purposely leave things for your new puppy or dog to chew on. You will find a huge assortment of toys for dogs at your local pet supply store. Choose whatever you like. You'll want a variety of things when you first bring your dog home. You'll soon find out whether he prefers to gnaw on hard rubber, a plush toy, a rope toy, a tennis ball, a chew hoof, or rawhide. Give him these last two in moderation. Too much rawhide is not good for a dog, especially a young pup. Gobs of rawhide have caused some dogs to choke, so it's best to give him that while you're home to supervise.

Phase 2

When you're home, give the dog or puppy more space to roam around. Close all the doors to rooms you want to remain off limits. But give him more room than you do when you're not at home. If you have children, close the doors to their rooms, as well as closing the door to the garage, the den, etc. Some houses don't have many doors. Maybe you want to close off the living room or dining room. Buy even more baby gates.

The idea is that the dog should only incrementally increase the amount of space he is able to live in as he gets a little older and starts to understand the rules of the house. Also, the less space you give him, the easier it is to manage him. You'll be able to keep a better eye on him.

DOG-PROOFING FOR AN OLDER DOG

You should proof your house for an older dog in much the same way for a puppy. You're not really sure what a new dog will do in a strange new environment. Better to take precautions. Sometimes they adapt quickly and easily with few problems. Other times, they're unsure of themselves and become nervous. They may resort to old bad habits in order to deal with any anxieties brought about by a change in their living conditions. Have patience. These dogs usually work out with a little love, understanding, and training.

SUPPLIES AND EQUIPMENT

Leash

It's best to actually have two leashes. The first one is your all-purpose leash that you'll use for walks around the block and most training sessions. Leashes or leads come in a variety of colors, textures, and styles. There are leather leashes, nylon leashes, and even chain leashes. The best by far (and also the most expensive) is a six-foot-long leather leash. You should have this leash for a long time if you take care of it. Leather is strong, wears well, doesn't stink, and is comfortable in your hand. Nylon leashes are also strong and come in a huge assortment of colors and patterns. They can even be monogrammed. Nylon leashes come in handy when you have to walk your dog in the rain and you don't want the leather to get wet. Or if you have to give your dog a bath and use a leash for some restraint. They dry quickly and don't shrink or crack. But they're not comfortable to hold; in fact, some may give you a rope burn if they get jerked out of your hand. Chain leashes are decorative and completely impractical. They're hard to hold, even if it's a look you like. But the choice is yours.

The second leash you'll need to buy is called a training leash. These are usually very long—8 to 10 feet. Many trainers recommend these as part of basic obedience class. Usually you would use it outside. You teach the dog to stay or come by working at some distance from the dog, letting the leash drag on the ground. If the dog races past you or won't come near enough, you step on the leash and then slowly wind the dog in, praising him as he gets nearer.

Flexi-leads are an interesting new twist in the dog-walking world. These operate like the adjustable clotheslines of bygone eras. However, you're holding the contraption, and the dog is at the other end of the line. The idea is that it lets the dog have some freedom to roam, but when he comes nearer to you, the line automatically withdraws and recoils. There is also a button which can stop the flow of the line at any time, so if you need to keep your dog close to you, you can limit the amount of line you let out. These leashes provide people with the opportunity to run their dogs with greater freedom in open spaces where dogs are not allowed off-leash. The only problem they present is a possible burn to those who come too near. If the dog encircles you, or someone you're with, the cord whips around and may cause a burn if it runs across your unprotected skin. You must be alert to any changes of direction or sudden activity on the part of your roaming dog. Overall, though, they're a handy way to have control and let your dog run.

Collars

Like leashes, collars come in a huge variety of materials, styles, and colors. Unlike the leash, however, one size does not fit all; you will need to buy a collar to fit your dog at his current size. Collars should fit snugly but not be too tight. You want something that goes around his neck comfortably and won't slide off the head, but you need to be able to insert two fingers between the collar and the dog's neck. Don't pull on the collar to make the space. It should be slack enough that it happens without creating too much tension.

There are four basic types of collars: *traditional buckle collars, choke chains,* the *pronged collar,* and *electronic collars.* The traditional buckle collar is a good first collar. These collars come in leather or nylon and have the traditional buckle fastener or a clasp fastener. They are adjustable, so your puppy should be able to grow into his buckle collar (though he will definitely grow out of at least one!). You can get a buckle or clasp collar in whatever color or style you want, from a conservative but elegant rolled leather, to black leather with metal spikes, to bright pink, to monogrammed, to decorated with ducks, hearts, or flowers. There are even buckle collars that glow in the dark! Your dog's collar can be a true expression of how you feel about him. Have fun!

The choke chain (now often referred to as a slip collar) is a metal link collar that is primarily used for training. Basically, this is a slip-knotted smooth metal chain that comes in various sizes. The idea is that as the dog pulls harder, the collar "chokes" him, pinching his skin slightly or impairing his breathing. To relieve the tension and breathe easier, he has to stop pulling. Used properly, this is not cruel at all and will save years of wear and tear on your arms and shoulders.

The pronged collar operates like a choke chain in that it tightens around the dog's neck as he pulls harder. But the pronged collar has dulled metal prongs that poke him in the neck as he pulls. Many people use this collar when walking dogs they can no longer control. These collars are especially favored by owners of large, furry dogs, such as German shepherds, Alaskan malamutes, and samoyeds, as sometimes traditional chokers don't always work on these breeds, they have so much fur on their necks. They are also used by people with very strong dogs such as rottweilers or Saint Bernards. Even if you have one of these breeds, you need some instruction before you start using a prong collar. Speak to a trainer or your breeder about whether it's the collar you need, or just more training classes.

You will also find a number of electronic collars in your pet supply store. There are electronic collars to stop your dog from barking, electronic collars to keep your dog within your property, even electronic collars to be used as training aids by hunters and people who work their dogs at great distances. The most commonly used are the bark collar and the collar that works with an "invisible" electronic fence. All work by "zapping" your dog with a burst of electricity when he barks, or tries to break the barrier of the fence, or you need to get his attention when he's far away from you. All should be used in conjunction with more humane training methods of teaching the dog to shush, mind his property, or respond to a whistle or voice command. They can definitely be abusive in the wrong hands.

Head Halters

These are essentially harnesses that slip over and around a dog's head, like the halters used on horses. The theory is that a dog can be led more easily by the head than by the neck (which is usually a very strong part of a dog's anatomy). These halters are very effective. But they have some drawbacks. First, they look like a muzzle, making poor Spot look like the canine version of Hannibal Lecter. Many people think they are cruel, because they make your dog look more dangerous than others because he's being muzzled. It takes some dogs a while to get used to head halters, too, as they can feel strange at first. But if you have a dog who pulls no matter what, you should try using one.

Food and Water Bowls

There is one simple rule with dog bowls: Make sure you buy bowls with wide and heavy bases that are hard to tip over. Especially with puppies, bowls can become playthings. You want to avoid letting this happen. With smaller dogs, obviously, you don't want to have too small a bowl. With larger dogs, make sure the bowl is not just bigger, but also a little heavier. Another consideration when buying bowls is what they're made of. You'll find stainless steel, ceramic, and plastic bowls, all in a variety of shapes and sizes. Stainless steel is the best because it's so easy to clean. You need two bowls: one for water, one for food.

Toys

All you have to do is go to pet and toy superstores and spend five minutes in each to know that there are almost as many toys for pets as there are for children. And you will have fun choosing from among them. Some of our personal favorites are things like Kongs, tennis balls, Nylabone Frisbees, and plush toys that squeak. When buying plush for a dog, make sure it's manufactured to take the beating that a dog will inflict on it. Kongs are cone-shaped rubber pieces that are seemingly indestructible, and dogs love them. Frisbees are a lot of fun, too. But most Frisbees, while they feel pretty strong to you and me, are made out of a plastic that just can't take the pounding that a dog's teeth can dish out. That's why the Nylabone Frisbee is the best. Your dog can play Frisbee with you all day long and not puncture it. It also has a little bone-shaped handle on the top, which makes it easier for your dog to pick it up. And of course, you'll want tennis balls for fetch. Tennis balls are especially good because they float in water.

As stated earlier, a lot of toys for dogs are edible, such as chew hooves and rawhide. These should only be given while you're there to supervise your dog, since cases of choking on the softened rawhide have been reported.

Crates

Once upon a time, using a crate was considered a cruel way to train a dog. Today there are still those who believe crates look a little too cagelike. However, the crate is one of the most popular of training tools, and rightfully so. Using a crate gives the owner a way to control his dog. And with a crate, the dog gets his own private "room" in the house. Let's consider some things. First, the dog is a den animal by nature. He likes a closed space which offers him protection and, when he wants, isolation.

Proper crate training starts with the right crate, correctly appointed. You want to buy a crate that will be big enough for your adult dog to stand up and turn around in. There are two main types of crates: wire and plastic. The wire crates fold down and can be carried. The plastic crates are typically referred to as airline crates because they're the ones that are used to transport animals on airlines. The wire crates are open and airy so your dog can see, hear, and sniff everything that's going on around him. Airline crates have only a front opening and some air holes for ventilation; they are much more denlike. One way that owners can make a wire crate more protected is by draping sheets or, in cold weather, blankets over the top of the crate. This shuts out light and drafts.

You might consider having more than one crate for your dog if you want a permanent crate for him in the kitchen as well as one to serve as his bed upstairs with you. Again, the choice is yours.

Whichever kind you choose, if you have a puppy and you've wisely bought a crate that will fit him when he's full grown, he is going to have a lot of room in it. This is not good, because he will be able to eat and sleep in one end and eliminate in the other, which defeats all your housetraining. You want to create a divider to put in the crate that will cut the space down to about half. As your puppy grows, you can move the divider until he doesn't need it anymore. You can use anything from stiff cardboard to plywood as a divider. Just make sure your puppy can't grab an end to chew on and devour it.

Once you've selected a type of crate, you want to create the perfect den inside it. The best thing to do while housetraining your pup is to line the crate with a thick layer of newspapers. This way if he spills food or water or has an accident, it's no big deal—you just throw away the soiled papers. Give your puppy a warm comfy bed by folding up an old towel or blanket for him to sleep on and putting it in the back of the crate. Help your puppy associate the crate with good things by feeding him in his crate. The first time you want him to go in, put his food dish just past the opening and let him eat from it. After you've taken him out after his meal and played with him, toss a toy or treat into the crate so he scampers in after it. Close the door behind him, tell him what a good doggy he is, and leave him. He will probably cry, but you have to be strong. He will soon learn that good things happen when he's behaving himself in the crate.

A word to bargain shoppers: Crate prices vary greatly. You can often pick up crates cheaply from friends, in the classifieds, or at tag sales, as many dogs outgrow their crates when they get older.

Beds

Let's get this first thing right out in the open: Your puppy should not sleep on your bed with you. You may want to comfort him and have him near you, but it's not a good idea for several reasons. When a dog sleeps on your bed, you're confusing him. Sleeping in your bed (or one of your kids' beds) with you tells him that he's an equal member of the pack, and that he therefore has as much say about things as you do. This certainly doesn't mean you should banish poor Puppy to the basement to "keep him in his place." But a cozy dog bed or crate placed in the bedroom with you or in one of the kids' rooms will be comfortable for your dog, and better for you to maintain the hierarchy. You need to be the Top Dog in your puppy's or new dog's eyes, especially in the beginning.

There are a number of well-made dog beds available these days, so you won't have to look long or spend a lot to find one that suits your tastes and Puppy's needs. Like collars, beds come in a huge assortment. They're filled with different materials, covered with different fabrics, designed for arthritic dogs, big dogs, tiny dogs, spoiled dogs. This is another area where you can have fun making yourself and Puppy happy. Beds are better than folded blankets or a carpet remnant. Remnants can't be cleaned as thoroughly, and folded blankets may end up being a play toy and will require your constant folding. The only recommendation about doggy beds is that the bed you choose should have an outer shell that can be removed. Many have zippers. Unzip that shell and toss it into the washing machine whenever it starts to look dirty or to stink.

Dog House

Usually these are made out of wood or high-impact plastics. These tend to be made for dogs who are outside dogs. If you're going to keep your dog outside, then you want to make sure the dog house is dry and has some sort of bed. People who keep active sporting and herding breeds still consider this an acceptable way to keep a dog, although experts today tell us that dogs want to be a part of the family unit and suffer psychological damage if they spend too much time alone. But what did you get a dog for if you're going to relegate him to life in a dog house away from his new family? The only justification of a dog house is if you plan on leaving your dog outside and exposed to the elements for any part of the day. In this case, a dog house will provide shade and shelter. Just be sure you keep it clean and comfortable for your dog and that your dog isn't being overexposed to heat, cold, or storms.

ID Tags, Microchips, and Tattoos

According to the American Kennel Club's (AKC) Companion Animal Recovery (CAR) Program, eight to 10 million pets stray from their home each year in the United States. Despite the efforts of shelters, animal control officers, and veterinarians, only a fraction of those lost are ever returned to their owners. Most of them end up as strays, and if they are lucky and don't end up under the wheels of a car, they get picked up by a shelter that may or may not be able to locate the dog's rightful owner. The fate of that animal depends on whether it bears some traceable form of identification.

Tags

The standard method of pet identification for years has been the good old dog tag. They are inexpensive and come in all shapes, sizes, styles, and colors; some even glow in the dark to be easily seen by motorists. The beauty of the dog tag is that it provides anyone instant access to vital information about your pet. The first thing people do when they find a stray dog is look for some form of visible identification to see who it belongs to. In most cases, that's a dog tag or other identification either hanging from the collar or imprinted directly on the collar itself.

Even the most caring, vigilant owner can slip up sometimes and forget to close a gate or garage door. We're stressed, we're distracted, we're only human. Perhaps the fault lies with a houseguest or their children, who may not be accustomed to having pets around the house. More often it's the gardener or pool service guy who leaves the side gate ajar. First thing you know your dog is missing. But if the dog has an ID tag with your phone number and address on it, Fido usually isn't a fugitive for very long.

People always seem to notice a dog on the loose, especially if he's soiling their lawn. Should your dog wander very far, though, and end up at the pound, his dog tags—ID or even an annual city license—are going to be his Get Out of Jail Free card.

Even so, tags are not a foolproof ID method. They can fall off collars or are immediately tossed by dog-nappers in the event your dog is stolen. Theft of dogs is becoming an increasingly common occurrence, especially with smaller dogs that are easy to snatch from a parked car.

More often, owners simply forget to update their contact information on the tag when they change their phone number, move away, or whenever they go on vacation. The latter instance is more common than you might imagine. People don't think about the fact that if their dog gets lost in Florida, where they're visiting Aunt Tillie for a week, and their pet's ID tags show a California phone number, no one will be at home to answer when someone calls to say they found your dog. It does no good to put an ID tag on your dog if the address and phone number are incorrect.

A lost dog needs more than his name imprinted on a tag to ensure he'll be returned to his family.

There are tags and then there are *tags*. The Pet Protector System has taken the ordinary dog tag to a whole new level of pet protection. Launched in 1996 by Liz Blackman, the company's president who has more than 20 years experience in pet rescue, Pet Protector has helped save the lives of countless pets. It works much the same as emergency services like 9-1-1 or MedicAlert do for people, with operators standing by twenty-four hours a day, seven days a week to help owners locate their lost pets in any emergency, any time, anywhere.

A yearly membership fee of $20 buys you the distinctive Pet Protector Tag that attaches to your pet's collar, the comprehensive pet recovery system that stands behind it, and peace of mind, which is priceless. The tag bears the toll-free number on the front and an individual ID number assigned to your pet on the back. Should your pet need help in an emergency, all someone has to do is dial 1-800-HELP-4-PETS to receive immediate assistance.

Pet Protector System provides a broad range of security services for your pet. Features offered include these:

24/7 nationwide service with live operators—When you dial 1-800-HELP-4-PETS, there is always someone ready and able to assist you with your emergency.

Toll-free lost-and-found hotline—Reuniting you with your pet quickly reduces the time and expense of worrying, searching, posting signs, and placing ads in the Lost and Found section of your local paper.

Easily visible on your pet—Unlike some dog tags, the Pet Protector Tag is eye-catching with its bright red lettering.

Works whether you're at home or away—Emergencies don't necessarily occur when you're at home. Pet Protector not only helps find the owner's pet but the owner himself. When your pet is found, they will locate you wherever you are by phone, pager, or through alternate contacts.

Emergency vet referral and treatment—Do pets ever get sick during normal veterinary office hours? Hardly ever. Medical emergencies always seem to occur at the least convenient times, either in the wee hours of the night or after office hours. Pet Protector will help you locate the nearest veterinarian that provides emergency service, should an unexpected crisis arise.

Travel protection—As with people, travel doesn't always agree with your pet. He may become sick when you're far away from home and the care of your regular veterinarian. Pet Protector will put you in touch with the nearest veterinary hospital, anywhere in the United States.

Natural disaster or home emergency assistance—Occasionally people are separated from their pets during floods, hurricanes, tornadoes, or other natural disasters. The only thing more harrowing than the wrath of Mother Nature is being separated from your pet and not knowing whether you'll ever see him again. Pet Protector can help reunite you with your pet in the event of a natural disaster or any emergency at home, on the road, or elsewhere that might separate you from your beloved companion animal.

For more information about Pet Protector or to complete an online registration form to receive the membership kit, visit the Web site at *www.help4pets.com.*

Of course, no tag is beneficial in helping you recover your dog unless securely fastened to his collar, which should also be securely fastened so it won't come off or the dog can't slip out of it. More often than not, a lost dog isn't even wearing a collar, let alone a tag when it's found. People can easily read the information printed on a dog tag, but it will only bring your dog home to you if the dog is actually wearing the tag when he escapes your yard. The tag must be kept on your dog at all times to be effective. If no one knows where Spot lives or how to reach his owner, that makes it virtually impossible for your Little Dog Lost to come home to you. Fortunately, modern computer technology has greatly improved the odds of recovering your lost pet.

Microchips

Having a chip on your shoulder can be a good thing if you're a dog; a microchip, that is. Having a readable microchip imbedded in your dog provides extra insurance that your dog will be returned to you in the event he is ever lost. In the decade since its inception, the practice of pet microchipping has reunited hundreds of thousands of pets with their owners. Several years ago, a Washington dog named Griffey was featured on the NBC Today Show as a testament to the benefits of microchips offered through a special program offered by the AKC (more about that later). Griffey was returned to his family after being separated from them for six years, all because of a little microchip.

The microchip is really a tiny computer chip that is programmed with an identification number assigned specifically to your pet. About the size of a grain of rice, the chip is small enough to pass through a special hypodermic needle and is implanted deeply under the loose skin between the dog's shoulder blades. If your pet is ever lost, the registration number on the chip is detected using a special handheld scanner. The dog feels nothing as the scanner detects a radio signal emitted by the microchip. Some scanners also emit a beep to alert shelter personnel, animal control officers, or veterinarians to the presence of the chip. An identification number appears in a viewing window on the scanner and is matched with the owner's contact information, which is stored in a database.

You can have the microchip procedure done at a veterinary office or at your local shelter or at microchipping clinics held in some communities. Cost ranges from $15 to $40, depending on where you have it done, and there's usually an additional registration fee to list the ID in the database, usually no more than $20. Shelters may include the registration fee in the cost of the implant. The most common brands of microchips used are American Veterinary Identification Devices (AVID) and Home Again, both of which maintain worldwide databases that can quickly trace the chip ID number back to you.

Many people wonder whether it's safe for the dog to have a microchip implanted in its body. The answer is yes, perfectly. The microchip is encapsulated in a biocompatible smooth glass material so it will not be rejected by the animal's immune system. The needle is inserted at such an angle that it doesn't gouge the skin but slips neatly under it. As the injection site heals, a protective layer of connective tissue forms around the chip to hold it firmly in place so it can't migrate or be passed through the dog's system. If properly inserted according to the instructions by those who are trained to give vaccinations, there should be no problems whatsoever for an animal that is implanted with the chip.

The chip is inert and self-contained. It has no battery, power supply, or moving parts that need to be replaced. It can be implanted in any age pet, from puppies aged five to eight weeks to seniors. It is operational for 25 years and guaranteed for the life of your pet. The microchip can never be lost or altered and can only be removed surgically.

It would seem that microchipping your pet would be his guaranteed ticket home, but as you are probably aware, modern technology is not foolproof. All microchips are not created equal and neither are the scanners that detect them. The most widely used microchip brands, AVID and Home Again, are easily detected by scanners used at most shelters, but other companies manufacture microchips that certain scanners may not detect. That can mean life or death to your lost dog if he is microchipped but that chip is not detected by the scanner in use at the animal facility. Another problem with microchips, is that not everyone who finds your dog may even have access to a scanner. Mrs. Pettigrew, who might happen to spot Spot from her kitchen window digging up her begonias, probably isn't packing a scanner in her apron.

In the mid-90s, Banfield Veterinary Hospitals, which are located in most PetsMart stores, introduced a microchip that operated on a different radio frequency than most domestically produced chips, which made it unreadable by scanners used in most shelters in the United States. The different frequency, which is recognized by the International Organization for Standardization (ISO) and widely used abroad, made the chips undetectable with the current scanners in use at most animal facilities in this country, placing thousands of pets at risk.

The ISO chip, used in 140 countries worldwide, is not the standard chip used in the United States, which has a radio wave frequency of 125 kHz. In Europe and Canada, animal welfare organizations already use a standardized scanner that is capable of reading all brands of chip. In the United Kingdom, where this type of scanner is employed, 47 percent of lost dogs are returned home to their families—a rate more than twice that of this country.

Some claim that the companies involved deliberately made their chips unreadable in order to corner the market and force everyone to buy their brand of chip. Whatever the case, thousands of pets were implanted with chips that were not detected by the scanners used at pounds and shelters. The result was disastrous. Many pets were euthanized before their owners could claim them, and countless hearts were broken. If you think your dog was implanted with an ISO chip, you might want to consider having him re-implanted with an AVID or Home Again chip, which seem to be the two most universally detectable brands with scanners currently used at animal facilities.

The outcry that arose from shelters and devastated owners over the ISO snafu has launched a movement toward a "universal" scanner. The Coalition for Reuniting Pets and Families is pressing manufacturers and marketers to approve the use of a scanner that can read all brands of microchips and to make this scanner readily available to every animal facility in the United States.

The Iams Company has offered to donate up to 30,000 scanners (a $5 million value) capable of reading all chips to shelters, animal control, and veterinary clinics. The offer is contingent on the willingness of all chip manufacturers and distributors to embrace the mass use of a standardized scanner. You can find out

more about the coalition's efforts and whether need ultimately tri-
umphs over greed at *www.ReadAllChips.com.*

Tattoos

Your dog doesn't have to wear leather and ride a Harley David-
son to sport a tattoo, but it won't say BORN TO RIDE or MOTH-
ER, and you don't have to take your dog to the local tattoo parlor
to have it done. A numerical tattoo is also a reliable method of dog
identification and can be applied by most veterinarians, although
some say that the procedure has been somewhat outdated by the
introduction of microchip technology. Breeders still routinely use
tattoos as proof of identity for their registered dogs. The problem
with tattoos is that they are not always easily located or readable.
They can fade or if you have them applied to puppies, the markings may become distorted or hard to read as your dog grows, but
they are still considered proof of ownership.

You must register the tattoo number yourself with an organization such as National Dog Registry, which keeps the number on
file and will locate you if someone happens to find your dog and
calls in the number. Without registration, which costs around $35,
the number is useless and that tattoo on Bowzer's bicep may as
well say BORN TO LOSE.

As with microchipping, tattooing is easier to do while the dog
is having an elective procedure done and is under anesthesia. If
the dog is already anesthetized, tattooing costs $10 or $15, but
if a special appointment is made, it will cost $35 or more. Most
dogs tolerate the tattooing process pretty well, which can tingle
or sting. Okay, it doggone hurts! If you've ever had a tattoo, you
know how it feels. If Killer is a crybaby, he may have to be sedated.
The tattoo is usually applied to the skin inside the ear or to the inner leg or tummy, where it can be easily seen. A leg or belly tattoo

is better insurance in areas where pets are commonly stolen and sold to research labs, because labs will not accept any animal that bears a tattoo.

PETS GET HOME FASTER BY CAR

Another program that helps reunite lost pets with their owners is Companion Animal Recovery (CAR), which was founded in 1995 by the American Kennel Club. CAR provides twenty-four-hour service for pets that are identified with a microchip, tattoo, or AKC CAR collar tag. The cost for Standard Lifetime Enrollment is $12.50 for microchipped or tattooed pets and $15.00 to purchase the CAR collar tag (enrollment is included in the collar package).

All animals are eligible for enrollment in AKC CAR regardless of microchip brand. The enrollment database, located in Raleigh, North Carolina, maintains records on pets from around the world and contains over one million microchip numbers and thousands of tattoo and collar tag numbers. Although dogs make up the majority of the database, you can also enroll cats, horses, birds, and other companion and exotic animals.

Any pet enrolled in the program can be reported lost or found through the toll-free number on the AKC CAR tag. Press 1 and a Recovery Coordinator will take down the information you provide, such as the pet's AKC CAR collar tag, microchip, or tattoo identification number. The coordinator will call whoever is listed as the primary contact immediately. If the primary contact cannot be reached, the coordinator calls an alternate contact or a veterinarian. When a contact person is reached, the Coordinator makes arrangements for the owner to reclaim his pet.

AKC CAR maintains close relationships with animal agencies, field volunteers, professionals, and pet enthusiasts. CAR also works in concert with other national identification databases as well as individuals and organizations in animal welfare and recovery to provide valuable resources for you in the recovery of your lost pet. For more information about the CAR program or to enroll your pet, visit their Web site at *www.akccar.org.* You can also call 1-800-262-7894 to request an enrollment form. Once you do enroll your pet, as with any form of pet identification, it is important for you to update your pet's record and keep your telephone number, address, and other vital contact information current. Don't forget to write the numbers down someplace where they'll be safe and you can find them quickly if you ever need them.

Hopefully, your dog will never be lost, but if so, until he learns how to dial a cell phone or use a GPS navigator to find his way home to you, tags, tattoos, or chips are his best bet for a happy homecoming. As you've seen, in addition to the aforementioned devices, there are a number of helpful programs and organizations available to help reunite you with your dog if he turns up missing. Whether you choose to have him microchipped or tattooed, it's *always* a good idea to keep him tagged. If your dog is no Lassie, to insure she always comes home, you might just decide to opt for all three.

CHAPTER 5

Basic Dog Training

HOUSEBREAKING

The first thing every new owner should know before bringing a dog into the house is how to teach him where to relieve himself. The good news is that all dogs can be housebroken. The bad news is that a dog rarely becomes housebroken by just being let out several times a day. This comprehensive housebreaking plan requires dedication—but it's simple and foolproof:

- Crate your dog when you can't watch him so he won't relieve himself (if you prefer, use another type of space, as long as it accomplishes the same goal).
- Supervise (umbilical cord or shadow) your dog when he is out of his crate.
- Feed him a high-quality diet at scheduled times (no treats, people food, or edible toys such as pig's ears).
- Teach him to eliminate on command.
- Clean up his accidents immediately (remove debris or moisture, then treat with neutralizer and cleaner).

❧ Never correct him after the fact.

❧ Keep a log of his habits (when and where he pooped or peed, and when and how much he ate and drank).

CRATING

Until a dog is perfectly trained, he needs a safe place in which he can do nothing wrong. So when you can't keep your eyes glued to your dog and monitor his every move, confine him to a place where inappropriate behavior—soiling, stealing, shredding, chewing, or scratching—isn't an option. Crating is good because it eliminates the risk that he'll damage woodwork, flooring, wall coverings, or cabinetry.

Assuming you ultimately want your dog to enjoy freedom in the house, crating is almost a rearing necessity. Crating is widely accepted by behaviorists, dog trainers, veterinarians, and knowledgeable dog owners as a humane means of confinement. Provided your dog is properly introduced as specified below, you should feel as comfortable about crating him in your absence as you would securing a toddler in a highchair at mealtime.

Whether the enclosure is a room, hallway, kennel, or crate, it should be:

The right size. It should be large enough that the dog can stand without his shoulders touching the ceiling of the crate, but if he soils the area, it's probably too large for him.

Safe. Homemade enclosures may save you money, but you would feel awful if he poked himself in the eye, stabbed or hanged himself, or swallowed wood splinters or material such as wallpaper or blankets because you ignored potential dangers. Make sure there are no protrusions or sharp edges, and no ingestible components.

Dogproof. If he is prone to chewing, scratching, or jumping up, prevent access to any woodwork, linoleum, furniture, counters, garbage, or windows so your home doesn't become a victim of your puppy's destructiveness during his training period.

CRATING INTRODUCTION

Allow your dog to dine in his new crate. Place him and his food inside and sit with your back blocking the doorway of the crate. Read a book until he's finished eating, then take him out. For his next meal, prop the crate door and sit at the opening with your dog and his food. Place a few pieces of kibble inside at a time so he is walking in and out to eat. If your crate has a metal pan, place a mat on it to provide good traction and reduce the noise caused by the dog's movement. To encourage your dog to go in more readily, arrange a barrier on both sides of the crate so he is channeled inside.

Next, teach your dog to enter and exit enclosures on command. Put his paws right in front of the opening. With one hand on his collar and the other pointing into the crate, command "Bed." Pull him in by the collar as you place your hand under his tail and behind his rear legs to prevent him from backing away. If necessary, lift him in. Immediately invite him out with the "chin-touch okay" and try five more quick repetitions.

Practice several repetitions of this routine three times or more every day so he goes to bed on command—without being enclosed. If you shut him in and leave him every time he is put in the enclosure, he may develop a bad association with crating. But when he learns to go in the crate on command as a result of frequent practice, he is more likely to also accept being enclosed.

If you reserve his favorite toy for the times he spends in the crate, he may actually look forward to crating as an opportunity to play with it. Leave food and water out of the crate; dogs don't need it in there and most will dump or scatter it instead of eating or drinking. Create a peaceful environment by covering the crate with a sheet or, if his tendency is to pull it in, surround the crate with a couple of stiff panels for a more enclosed, denlike atmosphere. Avoid leaving a TV or radio on because your puppy may become a victim of unsettling and noisy programming and advertisements. Replace that cacophony with white noise; the gentle whir of a fan puts dogs at ease.

Sometimes a dog will bark, yodel, whine, or howl when crated. Unless he is trying to tell you he has to go potty, ignore any noise he might make. Most dogs will quiet down if you act oblivious. If yours doesn't and you or your family members are losing sleep or sanity, startle him into being quiet. Try throwing an empty soda can containing a few pennies at his covered crate, clap your hands sharply twice, or anoint him with the spray of a water pistol between the eyes. You can also create an earthquake by attaching the leash to his crate and giving it a jerk as he barks. If he's keeping you awake at night, move the crate close to your bedroom door. This way you won't have to leave your bed to administer a correction. If you're using a leash jerk, attach the handle to your bedpost for easy access. Once he's learned to sleep quietly through the night, gradually move the crate back to the original location.

UMBILICAL CORDING

A crate-trained dog is not house-trained. Your dog is likely to attempt naughty behaviors when loose, and therefore he needs plenty of supervised exploration to learn the house rules. If your dog is out of his crate, keep your eyes glued on him or, better still, umbilical cord him so when you can't follow him, he'll follow you. This gives you the opportunity to cut short misbehaviors before they become habits.

Tie his leash to your belt on your left side. Give him only enough slack to keep him at your side without your legs becoming entangled. If he attempts to jump up, chew, bark, or relieve himself without your approval, you'll be able to stop him instantly by jerking the lead. You'll be able to train your dog as you tinker, work, or relax at home.

SCHEDULES

Most dogs leave their litter to enter their new home at about two months of age. At this age, the pups eat a lot and drink a lot. They have limited ability to control their elimination and no idea that it might be important. Feeding and potty times should be adjusted to help the puppy reach his potential in the housebreaking department as quickly as possible.

DIET AND FEEDING

Feed specific amounts of high-quality puppy food at specific times. If your dog eats on a schedule, he's more likely to potty at regular, predictable times. Pups should be fed three times a day up to three or four months of age, and after that can be fed twice daily for the rest of their lives. If your schedule requires you to be gone for six or more hours at a time, feedings can be disproportionate. Consider feeding a larger portion when you will be home for a few hours and will therefore be able to give him the opportunity to relieve himself.

We'll cover this more in depth later in the guide.

FLOOD CONTROL

With pups who urinate frequently, you might try restricting water. But before doing so, tell your veterinarian about your plans. He or she might want to perform some diagnostic tests beforehand to rule out bladder or urinary tract problems. In severe cases where, despite a clean bill of health, the pup still continually urinates, offer water only before taking him out to relieve himself. With pups who just can't seem to hold it throughout the night, withhold water for three hours before going to bed.

Don't necessarily put food and water in the crate with your dog when you leave. He will be more likely to have to soil if you do. Besides, most pups will dump the bowls and swim in the food and water, rather than eating and drinking.

ELIMINATION ON COMMAND

Understand how much *your* puppy needs to go potty and teach him to do it on command. When active rather than resting, you will notice a significant increase in the frequency of elimination. At two to four months of age, most pups need to relieve themselves after waking up, eating, playing, sleeping, and drinking—perhaps as often as every 30 to 45 minutes, depending on the type and amount of activity. At four months, the dog may be developed like an adult internally, but expect him to behave like a puppy. Most adult dogs can gradually and comfortably adapt to three to five outings per day.

Teach your dog to eliminate on command. This lesson is handy both when he is too distracted and won't potty or when he's on a surface that he's inclined not to potty on—for example, a kennel run, wet grass, or where other dogs have been. Others will go potty only if they're in a particular area or taken for a walk. By teaching your dog to eliminate on command, you can get him to go where you want and when you want, and simplify the housebreaking process. Here's how to do it.

Leash your dog and take him to the potty area. When he begins the sniffing and circling ritual which immediately precedes elimination, start chanting a phrase like "Potty, Hurry Up." What you say is unimportant, but it should sound melodic and should always be the same phrase. Use the same words for defecation and urination. After a week of chanting while your dog is relieving himself, begin the chant as soon as you enter the potty area.

HOW TO HANDLE MESSES

No matter how careful you are, occasionally inappropriate elimination happens. If your dog has an accident:

- 🐾 Never correct the dog after the fact. Do scold yourself by saying "How could I have let that happen?"
- 🐾 Startle him by tossing something at him or picking him up in midstream and carrying him outside to stop him in the act.
- 🐾 Clean up messes immediately. Remove debris and blot up any moisture, then use a cleaning solution, and finally treat the soiled area with an odor neutralizer.

KEEP A DIARY

Write down the amounts and times you feed your dog, and any unusual consistency of his stool. If you later encounter a training or health problem, your notes may make the solution apparent.

Also, make note of when you are taking your dog out and what he is doing. Document any accidents so you are alert to the potentially problematic times and can make needed adjustments. Take inventory of when your dog isn't going because, at least 90 percent of the time, he should go potty when you take him out.

A truly housebroken dog is repulsed by the notion of going in the house. Every consecutive hour your dog spends wandering the house, sniffing and exploring, without an accident brings you closer to this ideal, but anytime he uses the house as a toilet, previous good behavior is usually canceled out.

PAPER TRAINING

Owning a small dog offers lots of advantages. One of these is that if you don't want to have to walk him outdoors, you can teach him to eliminate on papers indoors. To start, get full-sized newspapers (not tabloids) and a 16-square-foot wire-mesh exercise pen, available from dog supply catalogs or by special order from a pet shop. Place the pen on an easy-to-clean floor and line the bottom with newspapers opened flat out. For one week, keep your dog in the fully papered pen anytime you aren't supervising or exercising. Then, put a bed in the pen and gradually reduce the papered portion to one full-sized newspaper, overlapping five sheets to ensure proper absorption. Once is he is pottying on the paper, open up the pen within a small room or hall. When he consistently soils on the paper, gradually give him access to the house, room by room, when you are able to supervise him. Shuttle him over to the papers if he attempts to go elsewhere. If he begins missing paper to any degree, follow the confinement and umbilical cording procedure described for outdoor training, except take the dog to the paper, rather than the outdoors, to eliminate.

Once trained, some paper-trained dogs only go on their papers; others prefer the outdoors but will use papers if necessary. You can paper-train a previously outdoor-trained dog and vice versa, but you'll avoid extra work by deciding what you want up front.

SOCIALIZATION

Congratulations on this great new addition to your family. Now, make sure you show him off. Not for your sake, but for his. This eminently important process is called socialization. When the socialization of puppies is neglected, they never reach their potential. They're less adaptable, harder to live with, and often less happy. A dog who's received frequent and early socialization thrives on environment changes, interactions, and training procedures. He is also more likely to tolerate situations he's accidentally, and unfortunately, exposed to—such as kisses from a pushy visitor or a Big Wheel riding over his tail.

Usually, the socialization process consists of providing a safe environment for your dog to explore. Concentrate on four areas: socializing your dog to people, places, things, and other animals. In unpredictable or potentially unsafe situations, keep your dog leashed. That lets you prevent a wobbly youngster from trying to pick him up, and you can keep him off the sidewalk as a skateboard zips by.

Socialize him to people, making sure he gets plenty of experiences with both genders and a variety of races and ages. Go to the park, a parade, the beach, outside a shopping center, or to an airport if you're bold enough to pretend you belong there. Occasionally, leave your puppy in the care of a trustworthy, level-headed friend for a minute, an hour, or a day. Your objective is to teach the pup to be self-assured in your absence; therefore, don't say good-bye or hello to the puppy. Treat the situation as a nonevent so your puppy is less likely to experience separation anxiety.

Think about items people carry and equipment they use. Expose your dog to wheelchairs, canes, bicycles, lawn mowers, Big Wheels, and roller skates.

Take your puppy as many places as possible so he becomes a savvy traveler who is accustomed to elevators, stairways, manholes, and grates. Acclimate him to walking on a variety of surfaces such as gravel, wire, sand, cobblestone, linoleum, and brick. Because some dogs prefer to eliminate only in their own backyard, teach him to eliminate on command in different areas, so weekend trips and the like won't be a problem. If you want to foster enjoyment of the water and your dog isn't a natural pond puppy, walk him on-leash on the shoreline. Once he is at ease with that, venture into the water. Gently tighten the leash as you go, forcing him to swim a couple of feet before you let him return to the shoreline. Never throw any dog into the water.

Let him get to know other animals—dogs, cats, chickens, horses, goats, birds, guinea pigs, and lizards. Often, upon meeting a new species, a puppy is startled, then curious, and finally some become bold or aggressive. For his own protection and for the protection of the other animal, always keep him leashed so you can control his distance and stop unwanted behaviors by enforcing obedience commands.

Whatever you are socializing your puppy to—animals, objects, or people—approach in a relaxed manner and avoid any situation that would intimidate the average puppy, such as a group of grade schoolers rushing at him. Be prepared for three reactions: walking up to check it out and sniff, apprehensive barking with hackles raised, or running away. No matter his response, remain silent. In the first, and by the way, best, scenario, he is thinking rationally and investigating his environment. Don't draw attention to yourself by talking, praising, or petting. Allow him to explore uninterrupted. This good boy is entertaining himself and being educated at the same time. If your puppy lacks confidence or displays fear, don't console him, because this will reinforce his fear. Use the leash to prevent him from running away. If he is still slightly uncomfortable, drop some tasty bits of food (such as slivers of hot dogs) on the ground. Most puppies will relax after a nibble or two because the uncomfortable situation has been positively associated with food.

If loud noises frighten your puppy, desensitize him by allowing him to create racket. Offer him a big metal spoon with a little peanut butter on it. Give him an empty half gallon or gallon milk jug with the cap removed and a bit of squeeze cheese in the rim to bat around. It won't be long before he is creating hubbub and loving it. Of course, if the clamoring drives you nuts, feel free to limit his playtime with these items. Also socialize your puppy to walking on leash, riding in the car, and being examined and groomed.

PUPPY KINDERGARTEN

Puppies have so much potential, curiosity, and intelligence. That's why puppy training begins the moment your dog comes into your house—whether you want it to or not. Soiling, biting, jumping, barking, and running are natural behaviors; as a new puppy parent, it is up to you to show him where and when those behaviors are appropriate and, more importantly, where they are inappropriate. Begin teaching and socializing your puppy as early as eight weeks of age if he is properly vaccinated and his good health is confirmed by your veterinarian. Although the techniques in this chapter are best suited for puppies two to four months of age, you'll find the information valuable when training older dogs, too.

Leash Breaking

Put a buckle-type collar and lightweight leash on your puppy. For 10 to 30 minutes, 3 times a day for a week, watch him drag it around the house or yard. Better still, attach the lead prior to playtime with another dog or a favorite toy. He'll step on it, scratch his neck, refuse to move, or maybe even scream, all of which you should ignore. Since many dogs like to chew the lead, you may need to thoroughly spray it before each session with a chewing deterrent such as bitter apple.

When he is comfortable about dragging the leash, pick up the handle and coax him to walk on your left side by carrying and squeezing an interesting squeaky toy. If he really fights you, attach the leash handle to a doorknob and let him struggle with that while you drink a cup of coffee. Watch him out of the corner of your eye to confirm that his antics aren't endangering him. Repeat the procedure for five or ten minutes at a time until he is relaxed before attempting to walk with the leash in hand again.

Car Riding

As soon as your puppy is large enough, teach him to enter and exit the car on command. Practice this by leashing him, walking him up to the car, and commanding him to go in as you give him a boost. Invite him out of the car by calling "come" as you gently pull the leash. Practice several of these, several times a day, until he goes in and out on command. Even before your puppy is ready for that lesson, decide where you'd like him to ride. Crating is the safest option. If it isn't the most convenient, try a doggy seatbelt, which is available at many pet shops or by mail order. Don't feed your puppy for hours prior to riding if he has any tendency toward carsickness. It is also a good idea to keep the air temperature inside the car comfortably cool (if you roll down a window, choose one that your puppy cannot stick his head out of). Additionally, you'll reduce the chance of motion sickness by avoiding bumpy roads and abrupt stops or turns.

Grooming and Examinations

This section addresses training your dog to accept grooming and examinations. As to the specific grooming procedures, techniques, and products to use, talk to an expert such as a breeder, handler, or groomer. The manufacturers of Oster clippers offer detailed booklets and videos on many breeds. These are available from Oster retailers. You can also refer to an all-breed grooming book such as *Stone Guide to Dog Grooming.*

Begin by acclimating your pup to handling of all areas of his head. Look in his eyes, ears, and mouth, and check out his feet (feel the toes, pads, and nails) and body (run your hands along his legs, underbelly, chest, and tail). Touch his gum line, his teeth (don't forget the molars), and inside his ears. Hold his collar with one hand so you can jerk it to settle a feisty pup. Open his mouth as you would do if you were giving a pill—gently grasp the upper jaw with one hand and the lower jaw with the other, fingers behind the canine (fang) teeth. Try all these things when he is standing on the floor and also when he is on a table or other small elevated surface such as the top of a washing machine. If possible, tie a leash to an overhead pipe or ceiling hook so that the snap hangs down just low enough to attach it to his collar to create a noose-like arrangement. And just like a professional groomer, never leave your dog unattended when noosed.

We'll get into more specific grooming tips later.

Mouthing, Snapping, and Nipping

During teething when pups are from three to six months mouthing is common. Natural though it may be, you must stop mouthing of flesh and valuables regardless of when it occurs, so that it doesn't become habitual.

Here are some tips:

* Keep your puppy leashed any time mouthing may occur (especially in the house), provide him with plenty of exercise, and encourage play with proper toys such as Nylabones and Kongs. Flavor the items by dipping them in broth for a special treat.
* Offer your puppy wash rags that you've wetted, wrung out, and frozen. Chewing on these relieves the discomfort of teething. Replace with a fresh one when it begins to thaw.

Correct mouthing by either:

* Screeching "ouch!", jerking the leash, and eliciting play with the proper toy.
* Using bitter apple spray on pup's lip line while gripping collar with free hand.

Correct chasing or nipping of children by never allowing unsupervised contact. Always intervene to curtail disrespectful, inappropriate actions from puppy or child. Attach a leash to your pup that will allow you to jerk it as the child says "ouch."

Playing Too Rough

Avoid rough play such as pushing and pulling, tug of war, and growling. Instead, get down on all fours, swing your hair, and pounce, or play retrieving games, chase, and hide and seek. If games get too rough or out of control, stop jumping and biting by saying "Ouch" as you abruptly leave the game. If you choose to resume play, do so only after leashing the pup. That way you can jerk the leash to stop the bad behavior and immediately continue your game.

Playing Too Rough with Other Dogs

Rough play among dogs is usually harmless amusement for humans and canines. If they're generally friendly and tolerant of one another, dogs or puppies rarely inflict injury. They will get noisy and animated: growling, barking, squealing, tumbling, and dragging one another by convenient body parts (such as ears and limbs) is common. Break up the game only if one of the dogs is being endangered, or if the play occurs in a formal living room or while people desire quiet. Don't raise your voice to break them up. Instead, leash one or both dogs and give a subdued command to stop, accompanied by a jerk of sufficient strength to ensure that they follow your request.

Chewing on Stuff

In addition to providing young, curious puppies with proper toys and exercise, it is best to puppy-proof your house by keeping intriguing items out of reach—eyeglasses, remote controls, laundry, plants, and dried flowers. Allow him to drag a leash or tie it to your belt to umbilical cord so you can correct with a leash jerk or bitter apple spray if he begins exploring the wrong thing, then play with an appropriate toy. If he is off-leash, distract him from inappropriate chewing with a sharp clap of your hands as you say "Hey!", followed by praise and play with an appropriate toy. Smear bitter apple cream on tempting woodwork. Confine your puppy in a safe place when you can't supervise him and teach the shopping exercise.

Shopping Exercise

Teach the difference between his toys and taboo items. Choose a word to mean "get that out of your mouth" (use the same word whether he has a finger, a slipper, or a dead rabbit). Place a number of personal items and paper items on the floor and allow your pup to explore. As he picks up a taboo item, command "drop it" as you jerk the leash, moving away from the item toward one of his toys. Get him to play with the correct item.

Even Good Puppies Behave Like Puppies

If you prefer not to learn firsthand about the dangers of giving too much freedom too soon, puppy-proof your house by keeping it tidy, keeping doors closed and personal items out of reach and, as a preventative measure, smearing bitter apple cream on tempting woodwork and electrical cords. Confine your puppy in a safe place when you can't supervise him. Finally, keep him leashed and correct while in the act of chewing, then encourage him to play with an appropriate toy.

Jumping Up

Some puppies have no desire to jump up. They're content to let you bend down to pet them. Others jump up either because they are very bold and sociable or because they've been rewarded for doing so with petting and attention. If you prefer your dog not to jump up, remain quiet and walk away from him, shuffle into him, or stand on his leash so it tightens just as he begins jumping. The last technique is particularly useful if people are unintentionally being too exuberant and allowing the puppy to jump up.

Jumping on counters and furniture is the result of giving your puppy too much unsupervised freedom too soon. Distract your untrained puppy every time he considers looking at the counter or hopping on the furniture: Toss a shaker can at him, clap your hands sharply, or jerk his leash even before he misbehaves.

Many owners of small dogs—myself included—don't mind jumping up. Still, it is important to teach the "off" command as described in on page 76, so the behavior can be stopped when necessary.

Digging

Avoid leaving your puppy unsupervised in any area that has digging potential. If he attempts to dig, use a leash jerk or sharp noise to distract him, followed by praise and the offering of an acceptable toy.

PROBLEM PREVENTION

Giving a puppy or untrained dog freedom in your house can be deadly. Natural curiosity and boredom could make them chew electrical cords, ingest toxic substances, or destroy valuables. When dogs are given freedom too soon, those that don't accidentally execute themselves often become homeless because of damage the owner is angry about but could have and should have prevented. Dogs are opportunists. This doesn't mean they are bad; it just means we're foolish if we walk out of the room, leaving goodies on the coffee table, and truly believe our dogs would never even think about touching them.

If you don't know where your puppy is, he is probably into something he shouldn't be. Save your valuables, your sanity, and your puppy by watching his every move, umbilical cording him, or confining him to a safe, destruction-proof area.

Some people unintentionally teach bad behavior. Read over the following most common mistakes and identify guilty parties if you like.

- Impassioned hellos promote hyper-excited greetings.
- Feeding your pup while you're cooking, eating, or snacking encourages begging, possessiveness, or an upset stomach.
- Putting strong-smelling items in the waste basket or leaving any trash can easily accessible invites garbage raiding (remember, a dog's sense of smell is much keener than ours).
- Not securing clothing, children's toys, and linens encourages stealing.
- Repeating commands teaches the puppy to ignore them.
- Lack of exercise and meaningful activity forces the puppy to look for outlets—such as digging and barking—to relieve his boredom.

Simple Commands

You can begin teaching commands and tricks when your puppy reaches eight weeks of age. Since puppies are sometimes too distracted to be interested in food, the following method explains how to use your hands and the leash to enforce your commands. The added advantage is that your puppy will learn to accept handling and restraint and therefore behave better for the veterinarian.

There are some general rules for teaching sit, down, and come commands: Use a buckle-type collar; give commands only when you can enforce them and never repeat them; praise your puppy before releasing him from duty with the "chin-touch okay" (step forward as you gently touch his under jaw and say "Okay" as an invitation to move).

Sit

To teach the "sit" command, put your dog on your left side, hold his collar with your right hand, and put your left hand on his loin just in front of his hip bones and behind his rib cage. Command "Sit" as you pull upward on the collar and push downward on the loin. Praise him, then release him with the chin-touch okay.

Down

To teach "down," follow the same procedure as described for "sit," except as you command "Down," pull downward on the collar as you use the palm of your left hand to push down on his shoulders or neck. When he lowers his body to the ground, pet his tummy. If he rolls on his side or back, continue praising, then release him with the chin-touch okay. If your dog braces and won't lower his front end to the ground, lift the paw that is bearing most of his weight as you push downward on his shoulder blades. If his fanny stays up as his front end lowers, simply keep your palm on his shoulder blades until he relaxes his rear legs and lies down so you can give him a tummy rub.

Come

Leash your pup and wait for him to get distracted. Call "(Puppy's name), come" and reel in lead as you back up and say "Good, good, gooood!" Kneel down to celebrate his arrival and release with the chin-touch okay.

Pass the Puppy

Get your family to join the program by leashing the pup when at least one other member is present. Have one person hold the leash while the other holds the pup. When the person holding the leash handle calls "Buddy, come," the other lets go so the pup can be reeled in as the trainer of the moment backs up. Then that person holds the pup and passes the lead to the next person. This exercise can be practiced daily for up to 15 minutes; if you all habitually use the same, consistent training techniques, the puppy will learn to respond to everyone in the family.

USING TREATS TO TRAIN

Most trainers want their dogs to obey out of love rather than because they were beaten or bribed. But since most dogs love tasty treats, food has long been used as a training aid. There are basically three ways to use food: (1) as a lure to get the dog to perform a task, (2) as a reward for completing an already learned task, or (3) as reinforcement for behaviors offered by the dog (click and treat training).

Most people use treats and body English as a lure because it is the fastest way to entice the dog to perform a task. But be aware: There is a huge gap between following a lure and obeying a command. To bridge that gap, learn how to enforce your commands with your hands and leash. This will also prove invaluable if your dog isn't interested in the treat because he's full or distracted.

If you would prefer not to use treats, don't. Though using treats can enliven a dog's response to an already learned command, it is not necessary to use food to teach a task.

CLICKER AND TREAT TRAINING

Clickers are often used for training service and trick dogs. Simply put, when the dog does something desirable, he is given a signal (usually a distinct sound) that the behavior is right, offered a food reward and, eventually, taught to do it on command, possibly without the food. This method has long been used to train a variety of species, including cats, birds, and monkeys. Many trainers use the click of a tin cricket to signify the appropriateness of a behavior. For instance, if the objective is to teach a dog to sneeze, the trainer would wait for him to do that, click the tin cricket and offer a treat or other reward. Because of the power of association, soon the dog reacts to the sound of the clicker with as much delight as to the treat. Therefore, if the dog is working far away or retrieving and can't be given a treat, the clicker communicates that he is doing a great job. Of course, many people do the same thing with the word "Good!" instead of the clicker. With animals who are unresponsive to verbal praise—such as rodents and farm animals—the clicker is an invaluable training tool, but a variety of methods are equally successful when teaching basic dog obedience.

PATIENCE

Dog training is an adventure of sorts: never predictable, sometimes elating, and sometimes tedious. Be optimistic about your dog's potential, but expect his progress occasionally to be slow or nonexistent. Don't, however, abandon your original goals and settle for meager results: Shoddy, half-learned obedience can cause annoying problems or allow them to fester. Many owners give up on training but later decide to give it another try—this time approaching it with far greater determination and achieving far better results. Whether this is your first time around or your last-ditch effort, recognize that a degree of frustration is part of the learning process. If frustration or doubt strike, keep training. You may be five seconds from a learning breakthrough. Don't let your frustration or impatience win!

Finally, learning anything new—including how to train your dog—is challenging, so show yourself compassion. Decide what kind of behavior you want and pursue it with patience and kindness.

PRAISE

With some dogs, a word of praise goes a long way. Others appear unaffected by it. Gracious dog trainers use lots of praise at the right time in the right way to acknowledge and congratulate specific actions, concentration, and worthy intent. Experiment with a variety of ploys to find what delights your dog no matter what his mood. Quiet, interesting sounds, combined with scampering movement, gentle pushes, and vigorous, light brief scratching with your nails usually elicits a good response. Whatever you use, your dog's reaction is the most important indicator that you are on track. Does your type of praise make his eyes bright and get that tail wagging? If he's bored by your technique, working to find out what he likes will improve every part of your relationship.

Never praise your dog if he does his work in a distracted or preoccupied manner; he may think you are praising his inattention. Instead, do sneakaways to help him realign his priorities.

TEACH ANY COMMAND USING TWELVE INGREDIENTS:

1. Decide what you'd like your dog to do.

2. Decide what clear visual or auditory signal you will use to initiate the desired action.

3. Give verbal commands using the right tonality, inflection, and volume (don't plead, mumble, or shout).

4. Preface verbal commands with the dog's name. The name and command should sound like one word ("Buster heel," rather than "Buster . . . heel"). Just one exception: Don't use his name in conjunction with the "Stay" command, since hearing his name implies he should be attentive and ready to go.

5. Say the command only once.

6. Make an association: While teaching, give the command as you make the dog do the action (for example, say "Sit" as you pull up on the collar and push down on the dog's rear).

7. Give commands only when you can enforce them—otherwise, you risk teaching disobedience.

8. Decide on reinforcement: How are you going to show the dog what to do? Unlike the other eleven steps, this will change depending on your dog's stage in training.

9. Show your appreciation with precisely timed praise.

10. End every command by releasing with the chin-touch okay.

11. Test your dog's understanding by working him around distractions before progressing to the next level.

12. Don't take obedience for granted. Dogs forget, get lazy, become distracted, and inevitably fail to respond to familiar commands. Especially if he rarely makes a mistake, correct him so he understands the rules haven't changed and neither should his behavior.

Chin-Touch Okay

Just as important as the cue you use to start an action is the one
you will give to end it. Release your dog from duty with a word
like "okay" or "all done." Pair this word with an outward stroke
under the dog's chin. Dogs who rely on a physical and verbal release cue are less inclined to "break" their commands. For the first
three weeks, step forward when you deliver the chin-touch okay to
make the dog move from his previous command on cue.

Exercises and Usage

Obedience isn't supposed to be treasured like a fine crystal vase
you admire and display but don't use. Anything you teach your
dog should be used constantly and consistently. Wear and tear
may not look good on crystal, but the more you utilize obedience,
the more positively ingrained in your dog it becomes.

Of course, you'll be using the "heel" command on walks and
the "come" command any time you need your dog nearby, and you
probably can think of all sorts of times to use the "sit," "down,"
and "stay" commands. Additionally, consider using your obedience commands for all these purposes:

Sit stay: Use to stop or prevent jumping up, fidgeting for
grooming, begging.

Sit: Use before and during petting to control shyness, ap-
prehension, or enthusiasm. Also use it if he begins to pester
people, kids, or other animals, before feeding, when you're
putting on a collar or attaching a leash, and at street curbs.

Stay: Use during mealtimes to keep him away from the table.

Rapid-fire obedience commands: If your dog has any tendency toward aggression when you approach him, make him come to you and execute a few commands for you. Also use rapid-fire commands if he has something you want him to relinquish, or an object he might get possessive over, to accomplish your objective without reaching for him or the object. Your lifestyle will determine how and when you use obedience commands. Regardless of one's living arrangement and lifestyle, a well-behaved dog is much more likely to enjoy a great variety of activities with his owner.

WAIT

The "stay" command means freeze in the sit, down, or stand position, and therefore is very restrictive. The "wait" command, though, allows your dog to move about, but only within certain areas. You can use it to keep your dog in the car or out of the kitchen. The only thing "wait" has in common with "stay" is that both last until the next direction is given, twenty seconds or twenty minutes later.

Step 1: Wait at Door

Teach the "Wait" command at doorways first. Choose a lightweight door and estimate how wide your dog's front end is. Open the door 2 inches more than that as you command "Wait." Stand there with your hand on the knob of the partially open door, ready to bump the dog's nose with it should he attempt to pass through the opening. Be sure never to shut the door while correcting. Instead, leave the door open with your hand on the door handle, ready to stop attempted departures with an abrupt and silent bump of the door. If necessary, butt him with a quick movement that makes it appear the door is snapping at him every time he tries to peer or charge out. Leash your dog so that, if your attempts to deter him fail and he successfully skips across the border, you can step on the leash and prevent his escape.

Step 2: Wait with Distractions

Practice at familiar and unfamiliar doors as a helper tries to coerce your dog to leave. Your helper can talk to the dog and drop food, but your helper shouldn't call your dog. As your helper remains on the opposite side of the door, engage in lively conversation to teach your dog that even when you are preoccupied, the "wait" command is enforced. When that lesson has been learned, you'll no longer need the leash.

Off (Get Down)

Teach your dog the "off" command if you want him to stop jumping on people, furniture, or counters. To enforce the "off" command:

1. Quickly bump him in the chest with your knee.
2. Jerk the leash opposite the direction of his jump.
3. Slide your toe sideways under his rear feet to take him off-balance.
4. Tap his nostrils quickly and lightly with your open palm. If your dog jumps on other people or when he isn't close by, always have him leashed so you can deliver timely corrections. Say "Off" a split second before the correction and avoid using the "down" command for jumping up if you say that when you want him to lie down.

QUIET

There are three steps to teaching your dog to be "quiet" on command.

Introductory phase: Teach the "quiet" command by leashing your dog and creating a situation likely to elicit barking—seeing a cat, engaging in ruckus play, being around children, or hearing the doorbell ring. Command "Quiet" when he vocalizes and distract him with a sharp jerk of the leash or a quick spritz of bitter apple against his lip as you hold his cheek to ensure an accurate spray. Praise him when he is quiet.

Correction phase: After a half dozen corrections, issue the command and only correct when necessary. Always have your dog leashed and bitter apple in hand before commanding "quiet."

At a distance: If you're commanding from a distance or when your dog is tied outside, kenneled, or caged, attach a long leash to him so you can deliver a jerk—from any distance—as he hears "Quiet." Though not as timely, you can enforce the "quiet" command by running up to spritz and leaving quickly. Some dogs are so pleased you've come back that they continue barking every time you leave, despite the correction. That's why remote corrections—whether launching a shaker can, spraying water, or jerking—are better.

DROP IT

Use the "drop it" command to teach your dog to release objects from his mouth or not to pick something up. Some dogs, and virtually all puppies, like to chew, carry, and mouth anything they can—hands, clothing, the leash, gravel, cigarette butts, landscaping timbers, tissue. Your first reaction may be to pry his jaws open to remove it, but if you do, he'll soon be prowling for another item to grab. Teaching "drop it" will reduce his scavenging tendency.

Accompany the "drop it" command with a sharp jerk of the leash, as you quickly back away and offer to play with an acceptable object. If your dog has something in his mouth and your jerk doesn't cause him to drop it, spray your finger with bitter apple and touch his gum with the sprayed finger as you issue the "drop it" command.

Leave It

If he hasn't yet picked up an item, but he's thinking about it, you can either use the "drop it" command or introduce a new command such as "leave it." In either case, when you notice him eyeballing a taboo item, give your command and a quick jerk of the leash as you back away from the item while praising all the way. This looks very similar to step 2 of the "come" command, but use the "drop it" or "leave it" command before he takes possession.

Social Skills

Overcoming Fear

For your dog's sake, ignore your natural desire to console a fearful dog. Whether his phobia involves inanimate objects such as garbage cans, loud or strange noises, other dogs, children, or places like the veterinarian's office, hallways or stairwells, reassurance only reinforces fear.

His fright will diminish if you insist he concentrate on something else. Give obedience commands in rapid-fire sequence for two minutes or until he is relaxed, or at least responding automatically to "sit," "down," "stay," and "come." Then initiate playtime by running, nudging, patting the ground, or talking silly. Continue rapid-fire commands if he seems preoccupied by his fear. Practice first in situations in which he's uncomfortable but not panicked, then gradually progress to greater challenges.

Trouble-Free Car Rides

Good car-riding manners ensure safety for both driver and dog. A dog who sticks his head out the window exposes his eyes to injury or, if you swerve or brake abruptly, he may fall out of the car. His movement can obstruct your view and that, along with barking or whining, can distract you. Reduce the chance your dog will develop bad habits like vocalizing and lunging by containing him during car rides. Also, in the unfortunate event you have an accident, he won't be thrown about the car or escape through a broken window and run into traffic. You'll appreciate the additional benefit of a cleaner car with less hair-covered upholstery and nose-printed windows.

Veterinary, Groomer, and Kennel Visits

These experiences are more pleasant if your dog is under control. Test and improve his obedience by using it as you invite him out of the car, walk around the grounds, and into the building. Hand him over to caretakers without fanfare and expect him to remain somewhat composed when he's returned to you. Especially when you venture away from home, treat the outing like a training session rather than a vacation from obedience.

CHAPTER 6

Nutrition
and Feeding

Not so long ago, when you went to the store to buy food for your dog, there were maybe two or three brands to choose from. If you even bothered to examine the contents on the label, it no doubt read something like this: corn, wheat, crude fiber, meat by-products. Probably neither you nor your dog really wanted to know what was crude about the fiber or what that mystery meat was, but if you scanned the fine print you'd probably have seen listed somewhere ingredients such as lips, hooves, and . . . well, never mind. Of course, the only thing the dog cared about was whether it tasted good, and that much hasn't changed. What has changed is how and what we feed our dogs.

Since then, food selections have improved and so has the science of dog nutrition. As the dog's status has become elevated to that of a cherished member of the family, we feed our canine companions as well or even better than we feed ourselves. Consider some of these taste-tempting selections from Merrick: Cowboy Campout, Wild Buffalo Grille, and Campfire Trout Feast.

While you don't set an extra plate at the table for Fido—or maybe you do—it's evident from the quality of food being dished out to the modern day dog that the Age of the Culinary Canine has arrived.

DOGS BARK AS THEY ARE FED

As with humans, a dog's nutritional needs change as it ages. You don't feed an infant the same kind of food you do an adult. The same goes for dogs. From birth to adolescence to adulthood to senior, a dog's nutrition requirements for optimum health vary with each stage of life.

These days you'll find a broad range of diets that are specially designed for the growth, maintenance, reproduction, and geriatric phases of your pet's life. Those who are in the know about such things call it *life stage nutrition*, and the concept behind this is that you should be feeding your dog the diet that's best suited for his particular age and breed. Seems fairly simple, doesn't it? However, as you'll see, dog nutrition is a bit more complicated than you might think.

CANINE NUTRITION ABCs

Like all mammals, dogs require certain nutrients in their diet to maintain optimal health and vigor throughout their lives. Among these essential and nonessential nutrients are six main categories: water, carbohydrates, proteins, fats, minerals, and vitamins. All have a vital function in the animal's body. Here's a breakdown, according to the American College of Veterinary Nutrition (ACVN):

Water is essential to life. Between forty and eighty percent of your dog's body mass consists of water. Perhaps that explains why

Rex is able to sprinkle every plant in the neighborhood and never run out of water. Maintaining that high percentage of hydration is why your dog needs clean, fresh water available to drink at all times. So, when you hear that familiar slurping sound at the toilet, you know it's time to refill the water bowl.

Carbohydrates aren't essential nutrients to life but are beneficial to its quality. They can be broken down into two major groups, sugar and fiber. Like you, your dog burns carbohydrates for energy. Those stores of energy come in handy when the neighbor's cat or a sassy squirrel wanders into his territory. However, if he consumes too much of a good thing, he'll get fat and have to join the low-carb kibble craze.

Proteins are large, complex compounds composed of thousands of smaller units that are called amino acids. The body uses what it needs of these to burn for energy, but any excess becomes stored as fat. Dogs require 12 amino acids, and these MUST be part of the dog's diet, although in what form he gets them doesn't much matter. Good sources of amino acids are chicken, beef, and soybean. The highest quality sources of protein are egg and liver. Some dogs don't like liver, so your fussy fur kid might have to get his aminos from somewhere else.

Minerals are inorganic components of the diet, usually indicated as ash on pet food labels. There is no dietary requirement for ash, but dogs do need the following minerals:

*Macro*minerals include calcium, phosphorus, sodium, chloride, magnesium, and potassium, which are required in fairly large quantities (grams) daily.

*Micro*minerals include iron, copper, iodine, zinc, manganese, and selenium, required in relatively small quantities (micrograms) daily.

Vitamins are nutrients that are either:

Fat soluble (vitamins A, D, E, and K), which are stored in the liver and body fat or;

Water soluble (thiamin (B_1), riboflavin (B_2), niacin (B_3), pyridoxine (B_6), pantothenic acid, folic acid, biotin, cobalamin (B_{12}), choline, and carnitine). Water soluble vitamins are not stored in the body and must be consumed daily. The liver stores its requirement of B_{12} in the liver, so this vitamin is not needed daily. Both fat soluble and water soluble vitamins are needed in relatively small quantities.

Fats, also known as lipids, are large, complex compounds that are composed of thousands of smaller units called fatty acids. Present in most mammals are the omega-6 fatty acids, which are linoleic, gamma-linolenic, and arachidonic. Of these the dog has only one, linoleic. As many of us are already aware, the body requires some fat intake to burn for energy, but consuming too much fat is detrimental to health and longevity, whether you have two legs or four.

Okay, now that you know what a dog needs in his daily diet, you may be wondering how to make sure he gets all of that good stuff in his food bowl each day. Fortunately, that's much easier than it used to be. There are more ways than ever to ensure your pet gets all the things necessary to stay healthy and happy.

THE DOG'S DINNER

Many people opt for commercial feeds because they are more convenient to store and serve and are usually less expensive than canned varieties, although there are vast numbers of pricey specialty kibble to choose from. With these and most other brands of commercial dog food, you can feel confident that your dog is getting an adequately nutritional and balanced diet.

Commercial foods come packaged in several ways:

* Dry kibble, sold by the bag, contains 3 percent to 11 percent water.
* Semi-moist foods, sold in pouches, contain 25 percent to 35 percent water content.
* Canned foods, sold in metal or soft plastic containers, contain 60 percent to 78 percent water.

Most discriminating dogs polled would agree that canned and semi-moist foods tend to be more palatable than the dry.

Regardless of which food you choose for your pet, you can feel confident that nutritional experts such as the ones at UC Davis Veterinary Medical Teaching Hospital in Davis, California, are diligently working to develop ways to improve the quality and taste of what we feed our pets. They are also developing diets that address diseases that develop in our pets.

For more information about pet nutrition and the various brands of commercial dog food, from Blue Seal to Waltham, visit the American College of Veterinary Nutrition Web site at *www.acvn.org*.

DOG EAT DOG

If your dog scratches constantly or gnaws at his paws, it may or may not be fleas that are biting him. It could be the quality of his diet that really bites. Food allergies can cause any number of maladies in dogs, including hot spots and other skin problems; inflammatory bowel disease, which causes chronic vomiting and diarrhea and can result in severe weight loss and anorexia; and even B.O. The offending ingredients in pet foods are the same ones people are commonly allergic to: corn and wheat. When you read the pet food label and see that the first ingredients listed are grains, rest assure they will be the ones in highest concentration in the food.

As with humans, there is a link between feeding your dog a nutritious diet and optimal health and longevity. Cancer and other diseases can be tied to a poor diet. No one knows exactly why, but more and more dogs are becoming afflicted with many of the same ailments that plague twenty-first-century humans, such as heart disease, colitis and other intestinal disorders, and diabetes. Could it be that we aren't the only ones adversely affected by the stresses and environmental pollutants we are subjected to daily? Or could the fault lie in what we feed our pets?

If your dog has health problems that have not been effectively treated through other means, they may be caused by hypersensitivity to ingredients in his diet. Yes, you may have to buy the more expensive prescription diets instead of the lower priced food, but isn't your best friend's health and happiness worth a few dollars more?

When Fido Is a Foodie

Is your hound too round? Does his belly drag the ground? A sagging gut and fat on his neck and legs is a sure sign that you'd better put your paunchy pup on a weight-loss diet. Another sign is that if when you go for a walk you have to pull him behind you in a wagon.

If you've noticed that your pet's waistline is increasing and he's not as svelte as he once was, it may be time to put him on a diet. A fat dog is a dog at risk of a whole doggy bag of health problems. Being overweight means he's more prone to injury and the extra pounds he carries place the entire body under stress, particularly his major organs and joints. It puts him at risk during surgery because the surgeon has to cut through layer upon layer of fat, which means the dog is under anesthesia for a longer period of time. It can also complicate post-surgical recovery and drug therapy. Some breeds are more susceptible to obesity than others, but all of them are masters of "the poor starved me look" and know how to wrap you around their dewclaws to get that extra treat or tidbit. Given half the chance, some dogs will eat themselves to death.

HOW TO SCORE YOUR DOG'S BODY CONDITION

This nine-point grading system was designed by Purina researcher Dottie La Flamme, D.V.M., Ph.D., to help owners identify obesity in their pets. According to Dr. La Flamme, when you run your hands along the sides of your dog's body, his ribs should be easily felt with a thin layer of fat over them. The waist (the area behind the rib cage viewed from the top) and tuck-up (the belly area between ribcage and rear end) should be evident but not prominent. Here is the skinny on what shape your dog's in, according to La Flamme:

1. Emaciated: Ribs, hips, and other bones protrude and are visible from a distance. Muscle loss is also evident.
2. Very thin: Bones are visible but not as prominent, and muscle loss is slight.
3. Thin: Ribs and top of spine may be visible and the pelvic bones prominent. Waist and tuck-up are evident. (Sight hounds such as salukis, Afghan hounds, and greyhounds naturally look this way.)
4. Underweight: Some fat is on the ribs with a visible waist and tuck-up.
5. Ideal: Ribs are easily felt and have a thin layer of fat. Waist and tuck-up are obvious but not exaggerated.

6. Overweight: Ribs have noticeable fat; waist and tuck-up are discernible but not prominent.

7. Heavy: Ribs are covered with a heavy layer of fat and noticeable fat deposits appear on the spine and at the base of the tail. Waist is absent or barely discernible.

8. Obese: A heavy fat layer completely obscures the ribs and heavy fat deposits appear over the spine and around the tail base. Waist and tuck-up disappear.

9. Morbid: Massive fat deposits are in the chest area, along the spine, and around the tail base. No waist or tuck-up. Abdomen protrudes, and fat deposits accrue on legs and neck.

If your dog rates either underweight or overweight according to this guide, consult your veterinarian or a dog nutritionist for the optimum diet for your dog. A dog's caloric needs vary with breed, age, activity level, and diet, and some breeds, such as Labs, mini schnauzers, mini poodles and cockers, are more prone to obesity than others.

HELPING ROVER REDUCE

First of all, before you begin any weight reduction program, take him to your veterinarian for a full physical examination. The vet will assess his condition and determine if any health problems exist.

- ❧ Cut down on the snacks, or if you just can't resist those pleading brown eyes, offer healthier, lowfat snacks.

- ❧ More and more people are getting healthier by exercising with their pets. It's good for both of you. Help your pet become more active and fit with long walks, play, or training sessions. A dog left alone in the backyard all day won't exercise himself, but two dogs might romp and play together.

- Choose nutritious but low-fat dog food and treats. Read the labels. An acceptable range of fat content in dry food is between 12 and 16 percent, but inactive dogs should get a lower percentage of fat than active dogs. If your dog competes in herding, agility, or other sports, he's going to need more fat content in his food than a lap warmer.
- Whether or not your dog has cleaned his bowl, pick it up after 15 minutes.
- Beware the garbage gastronome and counter surfer.

According to the Association of Pet Products Manufacturers, the National Research Council of the Academy of Sciences estimates that obesity will occur in 25 percent of dogs and cats; likewise, the market for weight-control pet food has grown by the same percent and is the fastest-growing segment of the pet food industry. As we've grown fatter, so have our pets. Someone once said, if your dog is fat, you aren't getting enough exercise. Joking aside, being overweight is as harmful for your pet as it is for you. Obesity is the cause of heart disease, diabetes, arthritis, and other health disorders that can cut your pet's life short.

The best way to control your pet's weight is the same as it is for you—limit caloric intake and get more exercise. It's actually much easier to reduce your dog's weight than your own because we control his food intake and exercise. If only we could get someone to do the same for us.

CHEF BOY R DOG

Cats aren't the only finicky eaters. There are many reasons why your dog may turn up his nose at just about every store-bought brand of dog food you set before him. For some dogs, nothing beats Mom's good home cooking. Dogs are natural born scavengers, and they'd rather have just about anything off your plate than what you usually put on theirs. Face it, if you've ever fed him table scraps, you may as well pull up a chair for him at dinnertime. Once he's tasted filet mignon, it's hard to go back to dry kibble. Would you?

Other reasons for getting creative for your canine in the kitchen might be if your dog has allergies to the ingredients in commercial foods, as previously discussed, or perhaps you're a health nut and prefer to offer your pet a holistic diet. Your dog may have special health needs such as a progressive disease that causes him to have a poor appetite. Maybe you're just a born chef who enjoys the culinary arts and would like to prepare your dog's meals, too, the way you do for the rest of your family.

You can find out more about cooking for the canine and try some of the recipes in these books by Micki Voisard: *Eat, Drink, and Wag Your Tail: Improving the Lives of Our Dogs Through Nutrition* and *Becoming the Chef Your Dog Thinks You Are*, or visit *www.dogchefs.com*. Another source is *Real Food for Dogs: 50 Vet-Approved Recipes to Please the Canine Gastronome*, written by Arden Moore.

If, for whatever reason, you go the homemade diet route, it's important to ensure that your dog will be getting the proper nutrition from his diet that includes all the essential elements a dog needs to maintain good health. Nutritionists recommend that if your pet gets more than half its daily caloric intake from table foods, then his diet should be specially formulated to ensure proper nutrients are present. Vitamin or other supplements may be necessary.

Consult a veterinarian or pet nutritionist to help you design the best diet for your dog's particular needs. We don't always get everything we need from our diet, either, but remember that this is not a little person but another species with different nutritional needs than your own.

THE BARF DIET

This may not sound particularly appetizing to you, but the Biologically Appropriate Raw (or Real) Food (BARF) diet has its devotees among humans and their dogs. As described in *Give Your Dog a Bone*, by Dr. Ian Billinghurst, the BARF diet consists mainly of bones and offal (internal organs), but Dog does not live by meat alone. This diet also includes vegetables, fruits, egg, flaxseed, garlic, kelp, alfalfa, and kefir, which is something akin to yogurt but with more "good" bacteria to promote a healthy intestinal tract. Everything is raw or uncooked, as it would be in nature for a wild dog. The premise behind this revolutionary, or rather *evolutionary*, diet is that for millions of years dogs fed on the remains of other animals, mostly bones, and that this instinct and ability endures in the modern dog. Bones, being a source of a wide variety of nutrients, enzymes, and antioxidant/anti-aging factors, should be a part of any dog's diet, according to Dr. Billinghurst, who is a veterinary surgeon in Australia.

Early on, when Billinghurst began feeding his own dogs a similar diet, he discovered an amazing improvement in their health and knew he was on to something. A key factor in his estimation was the elimination of processed pet foods, with their chemicals and cooked grains. From his studies in veterinary medicine and pet nutrition, and his experiences with his own dogs, he developed this unique nutritional approach that has been adopted by many breeders and has steadily gained a following among dog owners around the world since the publication of his book in 1993. He has written a second book, titled *Grow Your Pups with Bones.*

Critics of the BARF diet claim that domesticated dogs are not the same as prehistoric or wild dogs and point out that dogs do not typically live as long in the wild. Whether or not that is because of splinters in the intestine or intestinal blockages that can be caused by ingesting bones, no one can say. It could be that Fifi the pampered lap dog, who is only a distant cousin of the wolf that brought down and devoured mastodons, is the product of generations of inbreeding and that may have diminished her ability to digest bones. If you've ever stepped barefooted in a nasty wad of partially digested beef bone from the Sunday roast that she vomited up on your carpet, you'd probably agree.

As to what is the best nutrition for your dog, there are as many opinions as there are brands of dog food. But no one can deny that the importance of feeding our dogs the best diet possible is paramount to anyone who cares about them as deeply as their people do.

As with our own dietary needs, whatever diet you choose to feed your dog is a matter of blending sense and science to achieve the best recipe for your pet's optimum health and well being. You want him to be with you for as long as possible and enjoy the best quality of life while he's with you. Of course, no matter what the age or breed of dog, the ultimate approval rating for what you feed him is in the wag of his tail.

CHAPTER 7

Grooming

G rooming your dog is very important. Why? Because the more time you spend taking care of your dog, the happier, healthier, and (you hope) longer his life will be. Does Rover like getting a bath? Not always. Does Spot like getting his toenails clipped? Not likely. But both things are preferable to having stinky, matted coats that are infested with fleas or toenails so long they curl under and pierce the foot pads! These are extremes of lack of grooming, but things like this happen. Not to your dog, though.

The things that we'll cover include brushing, bathing, the importance of toenail clipping, and ear and eye care. These are grooming essentials for all dogs, even if your dog has very short hair. Grooming is not just about making Fido look pretty (do you think he cares how pretty he looks?)—it's about health maintenance. Why do you brush or wash your own hair? Because eventually, if you don't, it feels oily and dirty and unkempt. Washing your dog's skin and coat, keeping his eyes and ears clean and free from infection, and all parts of preventive health care will be discussed later in the guide.

A well-groomed dog will be happier, and you'll be happier because not only will your dog be cleaner—your vet bills will be smaller. With an overall grooming routine, you'll be defeating problems before they arise.

Surprisingly, most dogs are very resistant to baths, ear cleaning, and toenail clipping. They sulk through it at best and can actively protest at worst, causing you to throw down the nail clippers in complete frustration. To prevent this, approach grooming from a positive perspective. With a firm but kind hold on your dog, keep a happy tone in your voice. Barking the word "no!" all through one of these sessions is something akin to a nightmare if you consider the experience from his point of view. Have a little heart, be patient and firm, and you will go a long way to having a better-behaved and more cooperative dog.

BRUSHING

Why do you suppose many dogs stand by you all day long and let you pet them, but then won't let you brush them for a few minutes? Because maybe you're doing it wrong! More often than not the average owner is using the wrong comb or brush, especially in the beginning. Remember—a puppy has sensitive skin, and a spiky brush or hard comb wielded by an overenthusiastic owner can hurt! So be gentle and use a brush that's appropriate for your breed's coat type.

Brushing is a great thing to do. It helps keep the coat in good shape, which also promotes better skin care. Brushing also exposes things like burrs or mats in the coat so you can get them out right away, and will alert you immediately to the presence of fleas.

Brushing is also a way to work with your dog and examine his coat and skin more closely. If there are inconsistencies or infections or rashes, you'll see them a lot more quickly and be able to counteract them much more effectively if you treat your dog to regular brushing. In many cases, brushing is the time when many owners find out about things much more seriously wrong with their dogs, such as tumors (usually in older dogs) or melanomas.

Puppies

If you're going to start with your puppy, then begin with a strategy. With your puppy on a short (but not tight) lead, brush or comb him in long, even strokes, working from the base of the neck toward the tail. Stroke down from the top of the front shoulders toward the feet. Stroke from the bottom of the jaw to the deepest part of the chest. Brush the hairs on his belly (softly!) and on and around his back legs. Don't forget to brush his tail. During these sessions, you want to be making as many happy, cooing noises as possible. You're teaching your puppy to enjoy and welcome being brushed. If you enjoy it, chances are he will, too.

Adults

The same philosophy applies to brushing adults as to brushing puppies: Be firm, be gentle, enjoy it, and make it enjoyable. Use the right equipment, and cover all parts of the body.

You may want to include a flea comb in your arsenal of brushes. These are metal combs with very closely spaced prongs. Groomers and owners use these combs to go through a dog's coat. The prongs are so close together that they snare fleas in between them. When you come upon fleas, catch them in the comb, then dip the comb in some rubbing alcohol to stun and remove the fleas. When you're finished, be sure to put a tight-fitting lid on the jar of alcohol, or flush it down the toilet to be sure you're disposing of the fleas. If your dog has fleas, you need to consult the health section of this book and start a flea program immediately. Chances are your dog, house, and yard will need to be treated to remove them completely.

BATHS

Bathing your dog may not be one of the most pleasant experiences, but it doesn't have to be that bad if you once again employ patience, perseverance, and firm kindness. Before you wash your dog, it's usually a good idea to brush him, especially during the shedding season. First put cotton balls in your dog's ears to keep too much water from getting in them. Then wet down the dog with warm water. Start with a big gob of shampoo on your hands and start at the base of the neck, working your way along the body toward the tail. There are many excellent dog shampoos available on the market that are formulated for different coat types and different skin conditions and even to help ward off ticks and fleas. Just be sure you read the instructions carefully—some of these are not suitable for puppies. There are plenty of shampoos that are, so don't let that stop you from exposing Junior to bath time.

Continuing with the washing, as you work your way down the dog's body, rub in a circular motion. Don't be too rough. Make sure to work the shampoo into the dog's coat and skin under the chest and over his hindquarters thoroughly. Make sure you get the tail. Be sure to wet his head before applying a *small* amount of shampoo that you have rubbed between your hands. Cautiously shampoo his head and ears, being careful not to get soap in his eyes, which will sting. Sometimes it's safer to just give your dog's face a sponge bath without shampoo.

Rinse your dog with lots and lots of clean warm water. After bathing their dog in the tub, some people turn on the shower to rinse him off. A shower massage unit works well because you can take it down from its perch in the tub and basically hose down your dog in the tub. When you're done rinsing, let your dog shake himself (close the shower curtain if he's in the tub!). You'll towel him again and again and not be able to dry him as well as when you let him shake once in an enclosed area.

After the bath and a good shake, you have to dry off your dog so he doesn't catch a chill. If he'll stand for it, you can do what the pros do and use a hair dryer on your dog. This will fluff his flowing tresses and give him that just-primped look. Show dogs are so used to the bath and drying routine that they fall asleep while their owners carefully blow-dry and brush their fur into place. During post-bath brushing, much hair that hasn't actually come off (and lots does) with the water may have been loosened. A quick combing will make the coat that much nicer and keep that much fur from collecting in the corners of your house. When we bathe our dogs, we also take the time to wash the covers of their beds on the same day. Who wants a nice clean dog to go and lie down on something dirty?

CLIPPING TOENAILS

Why do we cut our dog's toenails? Because if we didn't, the nails would grow so long that eventually they would start to curl. When the dog steps down on his foot, the nails are pushed up at the base because the nails are too long. The dog actually walks as if he's lame. This is a tragic condition, and one that's so easily avoided.

When clipping nails, you have to be patient with your dog, and you have to be careful. The idea is never to get too aggressive about cutting the toenails. You just want to clip the end off, no matter how long the nails are. Even if they still look long after cutting off just the tips, don't worry. Ten days later you can get right back at it. That's because as you cut the toenails, the quick recedes. The quick is the inner, fleshy part of the nail, where blood flows and there are nerve cells. For dogs with white nails, you can see the quick (it's the dark shading about halfway up the nail). With black nails, you really can't guess where it starts in the nail. Best to be conservative.

What do you do when you have cut the quick? Well, there are different types of clotting agents that are available at the pet supply store. If you really don't have any of that, corn starch is usually pretty good. It also acts as a clotting agent. Try putting direct pressure on the wound, with a clean cloth. Make sure there's plenty of the agent or corn starch before you apply the direct pressure. The wound usually stops bleeding in a few minutes. If you just nicked the quick, the scary episode will be over quickly. However, if you do real damage, you might want to rush your dog to the vet immediately.

So, how do you go about cutting your dog's nails? Well first, you need to get the dog used to having his feet handled. Many dogs don't like this. Reassure him by asking him to lie down on his side, then pet each one of his paws, gently. Say nice things to the dog. Give him treats for his good behavior. Do this several times. Then, on the appointed day, have him lie down on his side. Reward him. Then take one paw at a time and start to clip. Remember, don't cut too far down. Just the tips.

EAR AND EYE CARE

Cleaning Ears

The first thing you need to know is that dogs with floppy ears tend to need more attention than dogs with cropped or short ears. Why? Because it gets hot and ugly underneath the ear flap.

Circulation of air isn't good in there, and the warm, moist conditions are perfect breeding grounds for bacteria and ear mites. Signs of ear problems are the three following traits:

1. Shaking head constantly.
2. Scratching ears often.
3. Stinky ears: you can smell them from here!

If your dog is showing (or emitting) any of those signs, then it's time to clean those ears. As with everything else, there's a right way and a wrong way to do this. The wrong way is to pry into the delicate ear canal with a cotton swab. The right way is to go to your nearest pet store and find a good ear-cleaning solution. Then go home, load up a cotton ball with some solution, and start gently swabbing the inner folds of the ear. Don't go too deep into the ear. Just swab between the crevices of what's called the outer ear canal. It might take three or four cotton balls before you're able to clean his ears out completely.

After you've cleaned the outer ears, squirt a small amount of the solution into the ears, hold the ear flap against the side of your dog's head and rub the ear around a bit to work the solution in. Swab off one more time. Read the directions to properly apply your particular brand. Afterwards, you and your dog will be much happier, and you'll avoid costly veterinarian bills from having to deal with ear infections. A note of caution: If the ear looks really red or raw and your dog is pawing at your hand in pain while you're trying to clean his ears, call the veterinarian. He's got a severe infection.

It's important to note that dogs who suffer problem ears tend to be repeat offenders. In other words, if your dog has had ear problems once, they are more likely to recur. Keeping your dog's ears clean will keep recurrences to a minimum.

Cleaning Eyes

The most important thing about the eyes is that they are the windows to your dog's soul—and his health. Your dog's eyes should always appear alert and clear (unless he's very old). In terms of hygiene, it's always important to wipe away the crust that builds up in the corners of your dog's eyes. While you might not think it bothers them, it does indeed. Left unchecked, it often is the source of irritation, or worse, may instigate an infection. Make sure to wipe your dog's eyes whenever possible.

Some breeds have large, protruding eyes that are especially prone to getting dirt and dust in them, and to risking abrasion and infection. These include Boston terriers, chihuahuas, bulldogs, cocker spaniels, and others. Some breeds, such as bloodhounds, have droopy eyes. These dogs, too, need extra-special eye care. Regardless of your breed, checking the eyes should be part of your dog's near-daily grooming ritual.

PROFESSIONAL DOG GROOMERS

Especially if you own a long-haired breed or a breed that needs a particular look, such as a schnauzer, a poodle, a Shih Tzu, or a terrier, you may want to use the services of a professional groomer for your dog at least twice a year. Professional groomers are very experienced and will make sure all the proper things are done to your dog. They are expert at clipping nails, cleaning his ears and eyes, and bathing and trimming the coat to near perfection. You may not recognize your dog after a day at the groomer's! There is no shame in leaving your dog with a groomer. You can't possibly know the many trade secrets they've learned from their years of experience and network of mentors and friends. Try them—you'll like them.

PART 3

DOGGIE LIFESTYLE
AND ACTIVITIES

CHAPTER 8

Dog Shows and Performance Events

DOG SHOWS

So, you're a consummate stage mother? Maybe you bought Fido because he came from championship lines, and you wanted to try your hand at showing? Maybe you've been to a dog show and it looks like fun? Or maybe it's just something you want to try once. Believe me, you're not alone. There are somewhere around twenty thousand dog shows per year, twelve to thirteen thousand of which conform to AKC recognized standards. Millions of people compete in these events, and an even larger number attend as spectators. This is called the "sport of dogs" by show people.

Now, first, let me caution you. Dog showing is very competitive. You are not the first yahoo who went out and bought a pet, and thought, "Gee, wouldn't it be fun to show Rover?" Dog-show people can be snotty. Many are very dedicated to their "sport" and don't take dabblers very seriously. In some cases, they actually loathe them. You will have to attend many shows in your breed before some of them talk to you without looking down their noses. Many will first ask you if you bred the dog yourself, or whom you bought it from. You have to understand, many people who compete are breeders whose livelihood, or at least some part of it, comes from dogs. You're just one more obstacle for them to overcome.

That said, there are also many lovely people in the sport, and the camaraderie and competition are fun. It's also fun because you'll be talking to many people who have dogs just like yours, and you'll trade all kinds of information and learn that much more. And the spectators are right there and also fun to talk to. They will all want to pet your dog and talk to you. And Rover will have fun, too!

Let's take a look at how shows work, and how the show world works.

SO YOU WANT TO BE A STAR!

Dog shows are not run by the AKC. Rather, they are sponsored by a specific organization, who will conform to the AKC's recognized standards. Now, you have to understand that breed clubs, such as the German Shorthair Pointer Club of America, are recognized by the AKC as the authorities on each breed. The club sets the "breed standard," and the AKC recognizes and honors that standard. The standards are modified over the years to one extent or another, to recognize new markings or colors, etc. One pending example is that the German Shorthair Club of America doesn't recognize black and white German shorthairs. However, these dogs are shown and confirmed in England, Australia, and in many other parts of the world. Someday, the club, and therefore the AKC, will allow black and white German Shorthairs into the show ring. This kind of modification is not that unusual.

OK, so now we're at an event. How does this all work? Let's follow a typical show as if you were a contestant. So, let's see, where are we? First, we'll compete at the breed stage. Do you have a dog or a bitch? That matters, because they're separated. Dogs and bitches compete in their own groups before they compete against each other. This isn't sexist. You have to remember, these shows are set up to reward good breeding. Essentially, they're very much like a livestock competition at a state fair. (Many dog people will not like that analogy.)

It is important to note that very little goes on at a dog show other than judging. The dogs will not be judged on talent, for example. If you've taught old Fido to shoot basketballs or to roll over and play dead, or some other fun, imaginative thing, then you're better off calling *The Late Show with David Letterman*, because the AKC doesn't recognize tricks.

The groups are each broken down into five major classes:

Puppies (6 to 9 months and 9 to 12 months)
Novice
Bred by Exhibitor
American-Bred
Open

The dogs are judged on general appearance, which includes things such as head, neck, forequarters, hindquarters, coat, color, gait, and temperament. The dogs are not judged one against another: "This dog is prettier than that dog." No! The dogs are each judged by a person well-versed in the breed who decides whether this dog is the best possible representation of what the ideal dog of the breed should look like.

In the next level, the winners are all brought in, and the judge picks out the best dog from all the winners. This is called the "winners dog." Several dogs are picked as "reserve winners." The bitch group is also judged in the same way. The reserve winners are placed in order of finish, as in horse racing—second, third, and fourth. These selections are made partly in case the winners dog is disqualified for any reason later on. The winners dog and bitch both receive points toward their championships.

In the next level, you start all over again. You're winners dog—you've won the group that showed. But now, in this next section, any dog that has finished his or her championship at any other show is welcome to compete. The competition is mixed now. Now, you go through the same exercise all over again. The judge looks over the field, where the competition is much tougher, and he or she judges them, putting them in some kind of order similar to what we just went through. At this point the judge picks a Best of Breed award. This can be either male or female. Then he picks a Best of Opposite Sex (in other words, he picks a male as Best of Breed, then he picks a female as Best of Opposite Sex, or vice versa).

Now, sometimes, if this is a breed-only event, that's it. The day is over. They showed German shorthaired pointers all day, and when the smoke cleared, you walked away with some big-time championship points, and Spot is thrilled. You're exhausted. However, today we are not at a breed-only show, so there's more to do.

At a full show, other breeds will be showing at the same time as you. All 144 recognized breeds are competing. You get a small breather here, and then you go back on stage. The next competition is the group competition. All the dogs were separated out by group—Herding, Sporting, Working, Non-Sporting, Toy, Terrier, and Hound. Since you own a German shorthaired pointer, you will be judged in the Sporting Group. The Best of Breed of each breed, that one dog only (and that's you!), will compete against all the other Best of Breeds who won in this group. In other words, you'll be competing against the Best of Breed of the golden retrievers, Labrador retrievers, etc. Again, do they pick these dogs because a German shorthaired pointer is prettier than a Labrador? *No*! An experienced Sporting Group judge will judge each animal against the ideal of what that breed should be. Each dog is rated against its breed's standard. Is this Lab a better representation of a Lab than this pointer is an example of a pointer?

Now, you were lucky to get out of the Sporting Group alive. Now, each group has been judged in the same way. So, here we are, and it's the final run around the ring. You are with the six other dogs who have won their groups. Yet another judge looks you all over, and in the same way the groups were judged, he or she chooses a winner, which will be crowned Best in Show.

You're certainly thrilled. What an exciting experience! And it only took a couple of days. You see, something as big as an all-breed show takes several days to complete. These shows are usually held outside at a large fairgrounds. The competitions, depending on the breed, can take all day. But if you like dogs (and apparently you do), then you just had more fun than you ever imagined.

HANDLERS

There are people in the dog-show industry called handlers. These people make a living showing other people's dogs in competitions. Many breeders use handlers because they cannot be all around the country, showing their many dogs. Some breeders will have more than one dog on the road. In situations like these, some breeders don't see their dogs for months and months at a time. They will sometimes fly into a city just to visit their dog and handler and watch the show, and then leave the dog with the handler and fly back home. This is the life of a championship dog for people who are serious about dog shows.

Now, it is a lot of fun showing your dog yourself. You drive to strange cities, stay in motels that allow dogs, and hang out with dog people for several days. It's this time spent with your dog that makes it the most fun. But if you are serious about winning, you may want to consider a handler. These people travel from show to show and know the many ins and outs of the ring. They know tricks of the trade and are very astute about the politics of the show ring. They are not cheap—they have many expenses to cover. Some of the recommended books listed in the back of this book will give you much more in-depth coverage of what you need to compete and win if you are serious about showing.

PERFORMANCE EVENTS

The AKC sanctions and different clubs sponsor a variety of events which are much more active than showing. These performance events are sometimes very general in their competition, and some are breed- or group-specific. For example, Obedience and Agility trials are open to all breeds, but you'd be hard-pressed to enter your Labrador retriever into Herding Trials, or your herding dog into a Field Trial event.

However, these events are a lot of fun to compete in. They do require plenty of repetitive training on your part and your dog's. However, if you like spending active time with your dog, it will give some structure to the fun you're hoping to have. And the competition, against other people who are having fun, too, is a flat-out hoot. These folks are not snotty at all. However, they are still very serious about competing and completing the titles that these events award.

These events are open only to purebred dogs. The various trials break down like this:

- Obedience Trials
- Agility Trials
- Tracking
- Field Trials and Hunting Tests
- Herding
- Lure Coursing
- Earthdog Tests

OBEDIENCE, AGILITY, AND TRACKING

We'll look at Obedience, Agility, and Tracking Trials first, because those competitions are open to all purebred dogs. The idea of obedience is to help meld you and your dog into a working team. This should be fun for both you and your dog, and will make him a better pet and you a better owner in the process. Agility stresses teamwork, expert training, and athleticism. And tracking requires not just a good nose, but an understanding of what is required in what might become a very serious profession.

Obedience

The idea is to be able to train your dog so that he can eventually be trained to comprehend and act on commands, regardless of distance or interference. This is the most popular of all trials among nonbreeders, as these are things which will make life easier for most owners. There are actually Puppy Kindergarten classes which will take dogs as young as three months. And there are pre-novice groups as well. Both these classes work with you and your dog on lead. In Obedience, there are three levels of increasing difficulty: Novice, Open, and Utility. In any trial, the dog must score 170 or more of the possible 200 points to earn his or her title.

Novice is the first group where you can earn a title. The title one earns is called a CD, which stands for Companion Dog. There are six simple tasks your dog needs to complete before he can have this title conferred upon him: stand for confirmation, heel on lead, free heel, long sit, recall, and long down. These are all off-lead.

Open is a little more difficult. The exercises required are retrieve (usually a dumbbell) over flat route, retrieve over high jump, free heel, drop on recall, broad jump, long sit, and long down. For completing this course, your dog will earn a CDX, which stands for Companion Dog Excellent.

Utility work is ranked as the hardest for good reason. These are some of the most advanced trials there are. There are five events: ability to distinguish between two scents, a signal event, group examination, directed retrieve, and directed jumping. If your dog finishes this course with a passing grade, he receives a UD, or Utility Dog, certificate. Of course, there are those overachievers who have qualified for UDX (yes, you've guessed it—Utility Dog Excellent) and even the OTCh (overall Obedience Champion).

Agility Trials

This is slightly more fun than obedience, but obviously not quite as useful. Agility teams you and your dog together as a pair to perform a certain number of tasks or exercises. It's a lot of fun to train and is very much like playing with your dog. The idea is that not only does Spot have to complete the exercise correctly (a feat in and of itself), but he also has to race against the clock. It can get exhausting. But it's very rewarding and often hilarious. The dogs seem to have more fun at these trials than in any other.

The dogs are broken out by size. No one expects a toy dog to make the same jumps as a Doberman pinscher. As in Obedience, there are levels. In Agility, there are four:

- 🐾 Novice Agility (the title you earn is NA)
- 🐾 Open Agility (the title you earn is OA)
- 🐾 Agility Excellent (the title you earn is AX)
- 🐾 Master Agility Excellent (the title you earn is MX)

Basically, your dog needs to complete an obstacle course. In order to gain the title, he must complete the course three times (at least one must be completed under a different judge). In these exercises, the dogs are required to run through and around poles, make a series of jumps, climb, balance, and race through tunnels.

It's scored very much like the Obedience Trials. The top score is 200 points. Infractions are deducted. This is fast becoming one of the most popular of all trials, first because anyone can enter, and second because it's tremendous fun. You'll laugh and be astounded. It's always an exceptional show.

Tracking

This is exactly what it sounds like. A course is made up over a large field or a series of fields, as well as across roads and through woods. A dog is given a scent and has to track that scent. The only thing is, in this case, the humans know where the scent is, because the judges mark the field. So when the dog goes off-course, the judge knows it. Sometimes while the judges lay the scent they create what are known as "tricks" in the field. They might make a hard right or left, or sometimes might crisscross a path with the scent. Along the path are things that must be retrieved and returned to the judges by the dog.

This competition is open to all breeds. It is surprising how many breeds participate. There are four levels of certificates, including Tracking Dog (TD), Tracking Dog Excellent (TDX), Variable Surface Tracking Test (VST), and Champion Tracker (CT). Of course, the various trials become more difficult at each stage. Many dogs that start out in this competition may go on to search-and-rescue work or police work.

BREED-SPECIFIC COMPETITIONS

These are competitions which more or less are aimed at groups. The Field and Hunting Trials are aimed at the Sporting group (and a few hounds); Herding is aimed at the Herding group; Lure Coursing is mainly for Sight Hounds; and Earthdog tests tend to be for terriers and dachshunds. However, if you have any breeds in these categories, or are just plain interested in dogs, it really is a lot of fun to go and see one of these events, let alone enter them!

Field Trials and Hunting Tests

Art Buchwald once said that he'd never heard certain colloquial phrases used with their real meaning until he went to his first field trial. Sayings like "That dog won't hunt" suddenly had new meaning. He also pointed out that some field trials were tracked by folks on horseback, because they covered so much ground so quickly, following the dogs. The crowd on horseback was called the gallery and was constantly pushing forward. The judges were afraid that the spectators might interfere, so once, one called out, "Gentlemen, hold your horses!" You probably get the idea—field trials have been going on a long time.

There are two distinct types of competitions. Field Trials are for pointing dogs, especially pointers (any kind), retrievers, and spaniels. The idea is that these dogs go into a field and spot game, marking it for their companion hunters and the other dogs. These are very competitive events. The dogs are tested and judged against one another. There are two titles awarded in Field Trials—Amateur Field Champion (AFC) and Field Champion (FC).

Hunting tests tend to be more open and involve many of the sporting dogs as well as beagles, basset hounds, and dachshunds. Here, the dog is judged against a level of performance. Although hunting tests are a little less competitive, they are still an excellent means of judging dog and hunter alike. There are three titles for hunting: Junior Hunter (JH), Senior Hunter (SH), and Master Hunter (MH).

Herding Trials and Tests

The relationship with herding dogs is one of the oldest relationships humans have. Herding trials exercises are used to gauge the development of what is still a very important job for many herding dogs. It's also lots of fun! The AKC separates herding dogs into four distinct groups: Shepherd (usually used with sheep and usually lead a flock); Drover (works livestock from behind, usually sheep or cattle); Livestock Guarding (they do not move livestock, but guard it from other predators); and All-Round Farm Dogs (these usually can respond quickly to different situations and can perform a number of different jobs).

The first few exercises are called tests. These test the general inborn instincts of your animal and his ability to be trained. After that, you're off to the pasture. There are six different levels to achieve.

The first two tests are Herding Tested (HT) and Pre-Trail Tested (PT). In these, your dog's abilities are judged, again, based on inborn reaction as well as certain trained functions. The next levels are progressively harder. The idea is that a dog must keep ducks, sheep, or cattle together, sometimes under very difficult circumstances. The four remaining certificates to be achieved are Herding Started (HS), Herding Intermediate (HI), Herding Excellent (HX), and Herding Champion (HCh).

Lure Coursing

This is probably one of the best spectator sports in all of dogdom. These are the sight hounds. Over an open, but rigged, course, sight hounds (used by humans to hunt over open plains since the time of the pharaohs), chase a flag at speeds which seem unimaginable. Yes, sight hounds hunt by sight. The dogs included are Afghan hounds, basenjis, borzoi, greyhounds, Ibiza hounds, Rhodesian ridgebacks, salukis, Scottish deerhounds, and whippets. A lure, or prey (which in most cases is a fluttering plastic bag), is pulled very quickly along a series of wires. The dogs give chase. The dogs are judged on overall ability, quickness, endurance, follow, and agility. There are three titles to be earned: Junior Courser (JC), Senior Courser (SC), and Field Champion (FC).

Earthdog Tests

Here's what the entry-level test for this is: Two large mice or rats are placed safely in a cage at the end of a long underground tunnel. Your terrier is let loose. The dog is judged on his desire to do everything necessary to get to those two rodents trapped in a cage underground. The rodents are safe, as the dogs cannot get to them. This is called Introduction to Vermin—remember, many of these terriers were called "ratters" and were used for ridding farms and factories of unwanted small vermin.

There are three earthdog titles: Junior Earthdog (JE), Senior Earthdog (SE), and Master Earthdog (ME). If you are a terrier person, you will marvel at this event!

OTHER OPEN COMPETITIONS

Some other competitions may be breed-specific but are not AKC-sanctioned. The AKC sponsors the Canine Good Citizen, which is an excellent program encouraging good canine behavior, and includes both purebred and mixed-breed dogs. Of course, there are other types of competitions. There are dog sledding events, protection events, scent hurdle racing, flyball, freestyle obedience (or canine freestyle), and Frisbee (or flying disk) events.

Canine Good Citizen

This is one event that the AKC sponsors that applies to all dogs, purebred and mixed-breed. The idea is that the dogs who complete these ten tests are certified to be good canine citizens who can behave themselves whether they're alone with their owner, with other people, or with other dogs. These events are usually sponsored by local clubs or community-minded organizations.

These are the ten tests:

1. The dog accepts a friendly stranger.
2. The dog accepts being petted by a friendly stranger.
3. The dog accepts inspection and grooming.
4. The dog demonstrates heeling while on a loose lead.
5. The dog displays that he can move through a crowd properly.
6. The dog completes a long sit or down.
7. The dog shows that he can immediately calm down after play.

8. The dog shows that he can accept other dogs politely, with no show of dominance.
9. The dog must react calmly to sudden distractions.
10. The dog displays that it can be left alone and still exhibit good manners.

If you intend on making your dog a significant part of your life (especially if you live in an urban or suburban area), then taking advantage of Canine Good Citizen testing is a very good idea. It's not only fun to learn and do, but it's valuable to be able to trust your dog and how he interacts with others.

Therapy Dogs

These dogs aren't in need of therapy—they help give it. They *are* the therapy. It's well known in the medical community that animal visits to long-term care facilities (nursing homes, mental illness facilities, etc.) often bring about tremendous reactions from the patients. Therapy dogs can usually get patients who are socially closed off to interact and help them to create personal relationships. In other words, therapy dogs are therapeutic. The dogs that make the grade for these types of assignments must be well-behaved and love affection. You need to have a dog that could pass the Canine Good Citizen test (though that is not a prerequisite).

If you enjoy doing nice things for others, many different therapy dog programs are run throughout the country. This is a great way to train your dog and help others at the same time. You both will feel better for doing it.

Dog Sledding

You'd think this one was popular only in Alaska, right? Wrong! More and more clubs are starting up all over the United States and all over the world. Many spitz breed fans have joined forces, and with the help of new technologies (sleds on wheels) and a devotion to the sport, have brought about new ways to train and compete with dog-sled teams in areas not covered by snow and ice. But here's the fun news—other breeds are being teamed up and are competing.

The premier guiding force in all of this is the International Sled Dog Racing Association. And they are all over. There are even some clubs as far south as Virginia and North Carolina.

Schutzhund or Protection Events

All right, for all of you out there who have heard about schutzhund, here it is. Schutzhund is German for "protection dog." Today, different levels of schutzhund training have been assigned to help qualify dogs for police work as well as for protection. This sport combines aspects of tracking, obedience, and protection. Schutzhund requires tremendous hours of training and requires a dog who is calm and self-assured. A hyper or anxious dog, one that lacks confidence or is easily distracted, is probably not a good candidate for schutzhund.

Although there are many people who are qualified for this type of training, the most notable dogs in this sport tend to be dogs used for police work.

Scent Hurdle Racing

If you have ever seen a relay race—for example, at a swim meet—that's basically what this is. The dogs are held at one end. On command, they must race over a series of hurdles, retrieve a dumbbell, and then leap the hurdles again with the dumbbell in their mouths, until they turn it over to their owners. Dogs usually compete two at a time in this type of race. Of course, some dogs, anxious to win their praise, either scoot under or go around the hurdles. They have to start all over again. It's so fast and so funny, it's no wonder this sport is growing by leaps and bounds.

Flyball

This is very much like scent hurdling, except that the dog, after racing over the hurdles, runs to a flyball box. Here, he depresses a lever that shoots a tennis ball up into the air. He must catch the ball, then leap the hurdles back. It's not uncommon for dogs to steal each other's tennis balls, or to fail to race correctly back to that starting point. But it is common for people and dogs to have a riotously good time at these events. The sport is governed by the North American Flyball Association, and it confers three different titles: Flyball Dog (FD), Flyball Dog Excellent (FDX), and Flyball Dog Champion (FbDCh).

Canine Freestyle (or Freestyle Obedience)

This is the weirdest thing you ever saw—but it's also very cool. It's the newest thing to hit the obedience circuit. In this competition, the handler and the dog have developed a very intricate routine that needs to satisfy a particular number of feats. The routine is then set to music. Sometimes costumes are used. Many dog people compare it with ice dancing. A horse person might point out its likeness to dressage competitions.

Frisbee (or Flying Disk) Events

This one isn't difficult to figure out. Many folks do this all the time with their pets out in the parks, right? Wrong! This stuff is fast, furious, and wicked. To see some of the top Frisbee dogs do their stunts and tricks, and compete against others, is as amazing as it gets. There are competitions all over the country.

CHAPTER 9

Traveling with Your Dog

ON THE ROAD AGAIN

In his famous song, Willie Nelson may have been singing about touring on the road with the boys in the band, but pet owners are singing the praises of a more pet-friendly world that welcomes their dog just about anywhere they choose to take him. It's no longer necessary to leave your dog behind with a pet sitter or in a kennel whenever you travel. According to a popular pet travel magazine of the same name, we've become a *Fido Friendly* nation as parks, recreation spots, hotels, and airlines have gone to the dogs. There's no question about it for dog lovers, travel is just lots more fun with a canine companion.

Globetrotting canines are not only welcomed in a greater number of venues and establishments than before but also treated like visiting royalty. Some hotels even offer room service for Rover with filet mignon on the menu, not to mention biscuits instead of chocolates on the pillow. There's no doubt about it, the dog days are here to stay.

From Cave Dweller to Couch Spud

Our relationship with the canine species, which has been evolving since 10,000 B.C., has advanced well beyond the scavenger lurking around the campfire, killer of vermin, or guardian of flock and herd. In fact, we've become *their* guardians.

"We are really seeing a change in the relationship between humans and their companion animals," says Dr. Rick Timmons, Director of the Center for Animals in Society. "It wasn't too many decades ago when dogs were kept out in the backyard, chained to the doghouse, tossed a bone, and maybe petted every once in a while. Before you knew it, they kind of worked their way into the house, into the living room, into the bedroom. Cats, of course, just came in the house and did whatever they wanted."

Dogs have been elevated from their once-lowly servile station to become our closest companions, our doted-upon darlings, even our surrogate children or grandchildren. In making their mark, so to speak, in modern society, they've staked their claim on our houses and our hearts. Nothing is too good for them.

Pet ownership is at an all-time high, according to the 2005–2006 National Pet Owners Survey conducted by the American Pet Products Manufacturers Association. For 2005, it's estimated that we'll spend $35.9 billion on our pets to provide them with the best food, shelter, and sundry comforts money can buy. Nearly two-thirds of all households in the United States keep a pet and of that number, 73 million are dogs.

Scientist and philosopher E.O. Wilson theorizes that humans have a need to be in touch with other living creatures and with nature. He says that we have become disenfranchised in our ur-ban environments. While our food may come wrapped in plastic packages, we still have the emotions of the primitive hunter and gatherer. The human animal's primal needs are not being satisfied by the concrete and skyscrapers that surround us. As our proximity to natural surroundings continues to shrink, our companion animals provide us with a vital link to nature. Perhaps that is why we long more and more to rove among what's left of the wide open spaces with Rover.

HELLO MUDDAH, HELLO FIDO

Pitching a pup tent takes on a whole new meaning when you take your dog to one of the many dog camps that have sprung up across the country. Located on the shore of beautiful Lake Tahoe in the Sierra Nevada mountains, Camp Winnaribbun provides an action-packed, fun-filled getaway on thirty-three acres of fragrant pine forest for you and your dog to explore and private beachfront so you both can frolic in the clear, blue waters of one of the most beautiful lakes on earth. Tahoe isn't called the Jewel of the Sierra for nothing.

Camp W, as it's referred to, offers campers the opportunity to participate in activities like obedience, agility, herding, tracking, and flyball as well as games, crafts, and photo sessions. It also provides health services such as homeopathy, psychocybernetics, and massage therapy, and of course first aid. Those of us who ever went off to camp as kids know it isn't without its occasional scrapes or insect bites. Like the summer camps of our youth, this one has the rustic cabins to sleep in after a day filled with nature hikes, arts and crafts and smores and, finally, storytelling around a roaring campfire. Best of all, it's a peaceful getaway for your dog and his best friend. For information on how to register for a fun-filled week at Tahoe's canine summer camp, visit *www.campw.com*.

There are other wonderful camps located in the East, such as Dog Scout Camp, which is situated among 300-year-old virgin pines in the beautiful Northern Lower Peninsula in Michigan. Their Dog Scout Motto is "Let us learn new things that we may become more helpful." Campers can even earn merit badges for completing activities such as sledding, search and rescue, freestyle, carting, tracking, lure coursing, and painting a picture, which can be matted and framed. Dog Scout Camp is something the whole tail-wagging troop will enjoy. For more on how to register, visit *www.dogscouts.com/camp.shtml.*

SEE SPOT FLY

According to the U.S. Department of Transportation, over two million pets and live animals are transported by air each year. More and more airlines are getting on board with the flying dog trend and are going the extra mile to make the trip safer and more comfortable for your best friend. In fact, Jet Blue Airlines was the winner of the 2005 Five Dog Bone Award from *Animal Fair* magazine for its pet friendly accommodations.

Whereas in the past, dogs were stowed in the belly of the plane along with cargo, now many dogs can fly First Class or Coach, right alongside their owners. United Airlines has even established a special Pet Class and offers frequent flyer miles and other perks for your pet. Midwest Airlines treats every frequent flyer Fido at check-in with two yummy organic carob chip cookies and a spiffy crate tag. Your dog can also earn a free round-trip ticket for every three round trips, six single flights, or by redeeming 15,000 of your frequent-flier miles. Midwest's pup pleaser program was the idea of Susie Kerwin-Hagen, a dog show judge who travels frequently with her own dogs.

Of course, if your dog flies with you in the cabin, he won't be sitting in the seat beside you watching *Best in Show* on the in-flight movies. He'll be tucked under the seat in a cozy canine carrier such as the Sherpa, the original soft-sided carrier, which was also a winner of the 2005 Five Dog Bone Award by *Animal Fair* magazine. Sherpa Pet Trading Company owner Gayle Martz named her company and her creation after her Lhasa apso, Sherpa. Martz is proud of the fact that it was her stylish but functional lightweight carrier that brought about the change in policy at major airlines about pets traveling in the cabin. It's approved for in-cabin use on Air Canada, Alaska, American, America West, Continental, Delta, Northwest, TWA, United, and US Airways and is recommended by veterinarians, the ASPCA, the Delta Society, and the Humane Society. There are many other carriers available as well that also meet airline guidelines. Requirements for size, weight, cost, and other regulations for carry-on pets are listed on individual airline Web sites or can be obtained by calling the airlines.

Obviously, not every dog can travel in the cabin with you. You can't fit a kennel for a Great Dane under the seat in front of you. Some dogs will have to travel in the cargo hold. Because of the dangers of transporting pets in cargo holds, the Humane Society of the United States recommends against it unless it is absolutely necessary to do so. Their organization has received countless complaints of animals that were lost, injured, or have died from extreme heat or cold, or suffocation due to lack of oxygen or rough handling while in airline cargo holds. It is largely due to such complaints that airline companies have adopted more stringent regulations, and cargo transport for pets has been greatly improved.

Rules and guidelines for transporting your pet on an airplane vary with each airline, but the following are some of the rules and guidelines that United Airlines recommends you consider before flying with your pet:

❧ Is your pet old enough? USDA requires that your pet must be at least 8 weeks old and fully weaned before traveling.

❧ Is your pet acclimated to his kennel? Animals travel under less stress if they are accustomed to their container before traveling.

❧ Is your pet healthy? Have your vet check to be sure your pet is fit to travel. You will also need a health certificate to comply with state and federal laws. It should be issued no more than 30 days before departure or if by cargo, no more than 10 days before departure.

❧ Have you selected your flight to make the trip as easy as possible? Whenever possible, book a direct, nonstop flight and avoid holiday or weekend travel, which might be busier. Also consider temperature; book morning or evening flights in the summer.

❧ Make advance arrangements. Advise the scheduler when you book the flight that you'll be bringing a pet, and it never hurts to tell the flight attendant you have a pet in cargo.

❧ If your trip is outside the United States, quarantine or other special rules may apply for some countries. Note that to be admitted to the European Union, all dogs and cats must have a rabies certificate and an implanted microchip or readable tattoo. Pets are not accepted in the cabin or as checked baggage to the United Kingdom.

❧ The USDA requires that your pet be offered food and water within four hours before you check in, and you must certify this in writing.

❧ The American Veterinary Medical Association does not advise sedation because effects on animals at high altitudes are unpredictable. Your veterinarian should decide if a tranquilizer should be prescribed for your pet. There are also some homeopathic remedies available that can help to calm pets when traveling.

🐾 Arrival and check-in—you cannot check in your pet more than four hours before the flight.

🐾 Certain snub-nosed breeds such as pugs, pekes, and bulldogs will not be transported if the temperature during the flight will be above 70 degrees F because of breathing difficulty.

Changes in pet safety measures during transit have been slow in coming, but in the wake of several tragic incidents associated with pets traveling on airplanes, federal laws are finally being implemented that require commercial airlines to report incidents involving loss, injury, or death of an animal during transport. The new rule, which took effect June 15, 2005, requires the airline to submit a report to the U.S. Dept of Transportation within 15 days of the end of the month in which the incident occurs. Before the law, airlines simply included these incidents in their lost baggage reports.

HSUS advises it's really best to leave your dog at home or in a kennel when you travel. Many people refuse to transport their dog by plane because of the risk of loss or injury and stress to the dog, but sometimes Fido just has to fly. If his owner is moving or if the dog competes in dog shows, it's fairly certain that his bags are packed and ready to go because he'll be leaving on a jet plane. It's ultimately up to a caring owner and the airline to ensure that Fido's trip is as safe and comfortable as possible. It's just plane humane.

BONE APPETIT

Continental canines have been accepted in and about eateries in Europe and Great Britain for years. Seeing dogs in English public houses is as common as dartboards and draught beer. You might even see a dog sipping beer when his master is distracted. French Poodles sampling *pomme frites* (sometimes referred to by les Americains as Freedom Fries) in sidewalk cafés on the Champs Elysées is trés chic in Paris, but Americans have been slower to set an extra place at the table for American dogs.

Because of stricter health regulations in the United States, most restaurants still do not permit pets inside or even in outdoor seating areas (service and guide dogs excepted). Since our canine friends have a tendency to be *au naturel* in their elimination habits, "Pass the Grey Poupon" could take on a whole different meaning in such a venue, which is why the rules are rather stringent about dogs around dining establishments.

FIDO FAST FOOD

With so many people taking to the road with their dogs, fast food restaurants could soon be adding something new to the drive-up menu—fast food for Fido. Could McDoggies be far off? How about Jack in the Barks? Most dog lovers would probably agree the idea is not too far-fetched. In fact, one former fast food executive, Kim Buchanan, came up with Fetch Fries for dogs.

You probably wouldn't be a bit surprised to learn how many people place an extra order at the drive-thru for the fur kid begging in the back seat. You've probably done it yourself. It may not be too long before you see menu selections like Big Mutt Mac or McFurry at the Golden Arches.

In the meantime, there are countless barkeries, pawtisseries, and doggy dining establishments across the country devoted specifically to canines. Bogy's Barkery, in Sacramento, California, is just one of many dog bakeries that offers homemade, organic treats for dogs. When Owner Jo Wardle's Chihuahua-Jack Russell mix, Bogy, became allergic to the corn and wheat in commercial dog treats, she started baking healthy treats and launched her own dog bakery. Wardle also hosts birthday parties for dogs, complete with a bone-shaped Barkday cake, pupcakes, hats, plates, balloons, and even gifts and treat bags for the pup parents.

Three Dog Bakery, a franchise with stores coast to coast in the United States and in Japan and Korea, also specializes in tasty treats for dogs. Browse online through their "Dogalog" to order everything from biscuits and bits to gift boxes and celebration cakes. You can even order monthly Dogliveries of yummies for your dog's tummy.

LET SLEEPING DOGS LIE

When you travel with your dog, finding dog-friendly accommodations is always a consideration, but no one wants to stay at a fleabag hotel. Fortunately, that's no longer a problem. Loews, Omni, Red Roof Inn, and Motel 6 are just a few of the hotel chains that have joined the Welcome Waggin'. Even five-star hotels and resorts worldwide are happily rolling out the red carpet for Rover, although that wasn't always the case.

"A couple of years ago, there were very few hotel chains that would allow pets," says Shawn Underwood, a communications representative for Petco. "Now they realize they're missing out on the market share because so many people are traveling with their pets. If they don't allow pets, those people are going to go somewhere else."

For dog-friendly lodging, you might also try Days Inn Hotels, like the one in Morris, Illinois, which welcomes four-legged guests attending the annual Basset Hound Waddle in the nearby town of Dwight. Every September, more than 1,000 hounds gather in the small, rural town for this off-leash, jowl-flapping drool-slinger's fundraiser to benefit Guardian Angel Basset Rescue, which rescued their 2,000th hound, Faith, in May 2004.

Don't be too surprised if you hear a chorus of mournful howls echoing in the hallways or share your elevator ride with some rather odd-looking, long-eared guests. Days Inn even hosts a Yappy Happy Hour in the hotel conference room for guests and their dogs, with refreshments for humans placed well out of basset-scarfing range, of course.

Letsgopets.com is just one of countless Web sites devoted to finding pet-friendly accommodation and other helpful pet travel information.

DOGGY ON BOARD

We've all seen them bounding back and forth untethered in pickup trucks, blissfully unaware of the dangers their owners are exposing them to. It's a sight that makes any dog lover cringe because you know when that truck brakes suddenly or is in a collision or even hits a pothole in the road, the dog can be thrown from the pickup into moving traffic.

Thousands of dogs are severely injured or killed every year when they jump or are thrown from the back of pickups. Laws in some states, including California, now prohibit carrying unrestrained dogs in pickups, although even a strong leash is no insurance against injury or death. If the leash is too long, the dog could strangle if it falls from the truck. If you must carry your dog in the pickup bed, place him inside a sturdy carrier or crate that is securely fastened down. There are also products such as the Puphut, a heavy vinyl awning that shields your dog from the sun, inclement weather, wind, and flying debris.

Of course, the best place for your dog is inside the car with you, but not sitting on your lap, where he can interfere with your driving and cause you to have an accident. Small dogs have also been killed by airbags that suddenly deploy in a collision. Fortunately for you and your lapdog, there are a whole new breed of pet restraints, ranging from harnesses to canine carseats, to keep your dog safe and secure. The carseats are cushy and comfortable but some also double as boosters and lookouts, so Fido can have just as much fun as ever watching the scenery.

More and more pet-friendly vehicles are coming on the market as public demand grows. The Jeep Grand Cherokee was a winner of a 2005 Five Dog Bone Award from *Animal Fair* for pet friendliness. Some features include pet barriers that keep the pet safely in the cargo area away from the driver and passengers; a Pet Seat Protector that guards seats from pet hair, spills, drool, snow, rain, and sand; and reversible floor carpets.

The Honda Element has a fully washable, highly durable interior that can withstand even the dirtiest, wettest dog. Saab also offers a broad selection of pet gear, including the Batzi Belt, a safe restraint that allows freedom of movement, a foldable travel bowl for those drive-thru bowser burgers, and an orthopedic pet mat. There are more products than you can shake a paw at for when you're ready to head out on the road again with your best friend.

Home, Sweet Home

Sometimes it's kinder to leave your dog behind when you travel, especially if the dog is old, doesn't travel well, or the trip will be too stressful, not just for the dog but for you, too. If you will be in a situation that is emotionally charged, such as a funeral, it could be distressing for dogs, who are by their nature highly sensitive to our moods.

There are still some places that are not dog friendly, and owners should think about how their pet will be received by others. Let's face it, not everyone is a dog lover. Pity those poor unenlightened creatures, but if fish and houseguests stink after three days, as the old saying goes, then a houseguest with a dog in tow stinks a lot faster, especially if that dog is ill mannered or poorly housetrained. If your dog is liable to chase the cat, bark at the parrot (which may bark back), nip at the kids, anoint the $3,000 designer sofa, or mark the Oriental rug (even the best trained dog slips up every now and then in unfamiliar territory), or if your host is allergic to dogs, make other arrangements for your fur friend while you visit. It'll be more considerate for everyone, and you might actually be invited back.

In certain travel situations you may need to pause and think about why you're bringing your dog along with you. You've probably seen dogs being dragged around anywhere and everywhere by their owners, even in very warm weather. Often the dog looks hot, tired, and stressed, and you wonder why his owner can't see that his pet would probably rather be at home asleep in an air-conditioned house on a 110-degree day.

Before you book that next flight for you and Fido or load up the pet paraphernalia in the Spot Utility Vehicle, ask yourself this: Is it for your benefit or the dog's to take him along with you on this trip? If it's really more about your happiness or amusement than Rover's, until there's a Six Wags Over Texas that's people-friendly, consider hiring a pet sitter or make other arrangements for your pet in your absence. After all, your dog's happiness, safety, and comfort are ultimately more important than having him with you everywhere you go.

CHAPTER 10

Pup Psychology

WHO'S THAT KID IN THE FUR SUIT?

We may treat them like little kids and even dress them up in silly costumes to look like miniature versions of ourselves, but make no mistake about your furry, four-legged friend wearing the designer dog sweater and the Bling rhinestone collar. Those domesticated creatures we baby talk, make smoochie faces to, and have welcomed into our inner circle are the descendants of wolves. They may perform tricks and tasks at our bidding and even mimic our own actions and antics, but like their wild ancestors, their instincts and urges are uniquely canine.

So, have a seat, if there's one in your house unoccupied by a dog, and I'll tell you a little about what's on your canine's mind.

THE LEADER OF THE PACK

Do you know who is top dog in your house? If it's Chompsky and not you, chances are good that there's a behavior problem or two in the household that will require some training, and you'll be the one who gets most of the training. People who work at animal shelters where millions of dogs (and cats) are surrendered each year can be frequently heard to say that there are no pet problems, only people problems. Uncontrollable dogs are the result of owners who, in the dog's eyes, have not assertively or humanely established the Me Boss, You Dog social status in the household. From the dog's viewpoint, you're both members of the same pack, and there can be only one leader of the pack. That pack instinct is deeply ingrained in dogs, and they need to know who is in charge at all times.

According to Cesar Millan, the Dog Whisperer, a dog's survival in the wild depends on the stability and strength of an organized pack where every member knows its place and follows the rules established by the pack leader. The pack instinct is a strong motivator, and to have a good relationship with your dog requires that you build a mutually respectful relationship with him based on the rules of the pack. That means the top dog in your pack had better be you or you could have some potentially serious problems on your paws . . . er . . . hands.

THE SOCIAL ANIMAL

The trouble usually starts early. Most pups are separated from their mothers and littermates at far too young an age. Responsible breeders keep puppies in their care for a minimum of three months before allowing prospective buyers to come sniffing around, but the majority of pups are sold at a much younger age. We've all seen the ads in the newspaper placed by breeders of questionable repute that read, "Adorable puppies, 6 weeks, ready to go in time for Christmas!" All pups are adorable, but until they reach at least 8 weeks of age, they aren't ready to be homed for the holidays, a traditionally hectic time which is not considered the best time to introduce a new puppy into the family.

A pup of only five or six weeks has not yet had time to learn the social lessons necessary to become a well-adjusted dog and a good pet. Puppies need to play and interact with their littermates and their mother to learn their social status and how to be a good member of the pack. They also need to be around humans who will handle them gently and accustom them gradually to human contact. Since they'll be living among two-leggers when they're grown, it's important to give them a positive introduction to this species that's so different from their own. Sadly, most puppies don't have that luxury and are sold prematurely into less than ideal situations.

Socialization is vital in order for a dog to develop a healthy disposition and sound temperament. Properly socializing your dog can be as simple as taking him for a daily walk in the park, or a stroll around the block. Take him different places and allow him to be around other people, including men and children. The growing number of dog parks as well as doggy daycare facilities and dog camps are also great places where your young charge will be exposed to other dogs of all sizes, shapes and ages. Off leash dog parks are popping up in nearly every urban community and provide a wonderful venue for socializing a dog. It's not so bad for socializing the humans, either.

"My Name is 'No, No, Bad Dog!' What's Yours?"

When it comes to training a dog, you need to accentuate the positive, eliminate the negative. Rewarding good behaviors is kinder and more effective than punishing bad behaviors.

When you command Rover to roll over, he does it because he desperately wants that Snausage or Canine Carryout you are holding up before him as an incentive to perform that task. When he completes the task and you praise him saying, "Good boy, Rover!" and hand over the treat, it's likely that next time you command him to, "Sit" or "Roll over," he'll do it because he knows that he's likely to receive praise or a reward for his effort.

We like being rewarded or getting a pat on the back for work well done, too, don't we? And we're likely to want to do a good job next time if we know we'll be praised for our efforts. Maybe Rover's a lot more human than we give him credit for.

TRAIN HUMANE

Choke, pinch, spike, shock. No, I'm not talking about the treatment of victims of the Spanish Inquisition but about widely used methods of dog training. Are these the kinds of things you should do to your best friend? The San Francisco Society for the Prevention of Cruelty to Animals (SFSPCA) doesn't think so. According to the SFSPCA, choke and shock collars may stop the dog from pulling or barking, but that's only because *it hurts*. In some cases, they say the dogs not only do not respond to the collars but also become desensitized to them to the point where injurious levels of force are required to make the dog respond at all. More often than not these pain chains are used incorrectly, making them ineffective and cruel. In the society's estimation, strangling a dog to the point of damaging its trachea is not training; it's abuse. If humans were subjected to some of the same "training" methods used on a dog, it would be called torture.

The SFSPCA believes that it is possible and preferable to train a dog without inflicting pain and that using halter and reward-based training is far more effective and beneficial to the animal. That's what they use to train their shelter dogs, and they say that the dogs make progress much quicker than with other methods. A well-trained and humanely trained dog is an adoptable dog.

TRAINING IS A SNAP WITH JUST A CLICK

Dogs are masters at reading our body language. They constantly pick up on cues, both visual and auditory. Dogs can even mimic human body movements and expressions such as shaking hands, slapping a high-five (or is it a high-four?), smiling, singing, and even dancing, one of the newer dog agility sports.

Your dog knows when you're leaving the house almost before you do. He immediately notices your hurried pace as you dash about the house collecting your things. He gets that hangdog expression that makes you feel so guilty because he knows that this time you're leaving him for more than just a few hours.

The dog is a master empath. He knows when you're happy and when you're sad and even seems to share those emotions with you. Have you ever had a dog place his paw on your hand or respond to you in some other way when you're distressed? If you had a dog during the bumps and bruises of childhood, you have known the comfort a dog can give. Some dogs have been known to laugh or cry real tears right along with their owners.

And we all know how keen those ears are. From the other end of the house, your dog not only hears and responds with gusto to the front doorbell (or even one on TV) or the clank of the mail slot but also hears the squeak of the refrigerator door opening or the faintest crinkle of plastic wrap, no matter how quietly we try to unwrap that block of cheese. What better candidate could there be for clicker obedience training?

The clicker is one of the most effective methods of training used to reinforce a positive behavior. According to trainers at K-9 Insight Obedience, of Planet Pooch in Redwood City, California, clicker training is based on the premise of *operant conditioning*; that is, forming an association in the dog's mind between a behavior and its consequences. When the desired behavior is performed, the trainer presses a hand-held clicker that emits a high-pitched sound, which serves as a marker. When the dog hears the clicker snap, he knows that he did something good and that a reward is at hand, or rather in his master's hand.

ARE YOU BARKING AT ME?

Long before Mr. Ed, the talking horse, whinnied his first words to Wilbur, people have wanted to understand animal language. This is especially true of dog lovers. Over the past 10,000 years or so, humans have learned to read canine body language with some degree of success. Or have we? Considering that there are almost 5 million dog bite victims in the United States annually, not always from someone else's dog, this may not be the case. A wagging tail means the dog is friendly, or does it? Experts tell us that whether the dog is friend or foe depends more on the position and speed of the tail wag, the set of the ears, and other body signals and, of course, the dog's primary means of communication, its bark. But how do we translate what is really on our canine companion's mind?

A couple of Christmases ago, Tessie Fell came to Three Dog Bakery in Sutter Creek, California, to buy a sweater for her chihuahua, Bruno. When she spotted Bow-Lingual, the Dog Translator, she was immediately intrigued. Retailing at around $120 and available in red or blue, the apparatus was considerably more expensive than the sweater, but what dog owner wouldn't want to know what her dog is saying? "That day I took it home, and I put it on him," Fell says. "He was sitting in a chair jumping up and down barking at me, and the Bow-Lingual said, 'Resistance is futile.'"

In another instance of interspecies communication with Bruno using the Bow-Lingual, Fell says, "I had walked in the bedroom and closed the door behind me so he couldn't go in there. He barked, and it said, 'Are you my friend or my enemy?'" Before long, her "chihuahua with attitude" was *talking* her ears off.

The battery-operated Bow-Lingual is easy enough to use. "The instructions are really straight-forward," Fell says. First you enter some information about your dog, such as size, sex, and breed. Then you attach a wireless microphone to your dog's collar and when the dog barks, a handheld device displays the translation. It even has a Home Alone mode so you can monitor your dog's barks and behavior while you are away. Other modes offer training tips and a health check to help alert you to signs of illness in your pet. All this is great, you say, but how does the Bow-Lingual translate what your dog is saying?

Paraphrasing from the Bow-Lingual User Manual, the Animal Emotion Analysis System, developed by Dr. Matsumi Suzuki of the Japan Acoustics Laboratory, is the result of many years of studying acoustics and animal behavior. From his research on dolphins, which use sounds to express emotion, he applied his findings to analyze how dogs communicate using barks.

Dr. Suzuki's studies consisted of collecting and analyzing thousands of barks from over eighty dog breeds, visiting homes of dog owners, videotaping dog behavior, and digitally recording their vocalizations in various situations. He then used an FFT analyzer, which breaks down sounds into their frequency components. He discovered through his extensive analysis that dog barks fall into six distinct patterns: happy, sad, on-guard/territorial, frustrated, assertive/playful, and needy.

Now, here's where things get really technical. A "sad" bark lasts .2 to .3 seconds with a strong component in the 5000hz range (no lower than 3000hz), whereas an angry or "on-guard" bark has "a clear, non-harmonic, fundamental frequency in the 250–8000hz range; a strong frequency component of approximately 1000hz, followed by fundamental frequencies in the 240–360hz range: a clear harmonic wave of up to 1500hz and a harmonic wave of up to 8000hz lasting .8 to 1.5 seconds."

Is this science or science fiction? The fact that the Bow-Lingual is manufactured by Takara Corporation, Japan's second-largest toy company, doesn't lend much credence to all that scientific jargon, but it sure sounds impressive to someone who thinks he's going to be able to talk to his dog if he buys one.

Other studies on barking dogs, such as the one conducted by Dr. Sophia Yin, debunked Takara's claims. After testing the Bow-Lingual repeatedly in identical situations on her Australian cattle dog, Zoë, Yin found that the precision of the device's mood translation dropped from 80 percent accuracy to only 65 percent. Although in some situations, such as doorbell response, isolation, or play, the results were accurate 100 percent of the time; however, the mood never varied. Yin states that according to the Bow-Lingual, Zoë is *always* frustrated. Knowing the high-toned temperament of this energetic herding breed, that unwavering mood assessment may not be too far afield, but Yin found the nonsensical translations of the Bow-Lingual such as "I've got a funny feeling" and "You just don't get it" fairly useless for her studies.

Whether intended to inform or entertain, the Bow-Lingual phrases are a barrel of laughs for the dog's owner. Yin offers a test on interpreting dog barks and even a bark survey for owners of barkaholic dogs on her "Barking in Dogs" Web site, *http://nerdbook.com/sophia/barking.html*. She explains, "While it's possible that a dog could be frustrated in all three situations, scientists determine the meaning of vocalizations by looking at the context, body posture of the barking dog, and the response of the animals or humans who hear the barks." Most animal communicators would agree.

Is this clever gadget a bona fide translation tool or the ultimate dog toy? Opinions are as varied as the dogs themselves. If you're like most dog fanciers, you're eager to know what Spot is saying or Fido is feeling and might want to give the Bow-Lingual a try. Although its popularity was short-lived in the United States, it may still be available in some pet stores, or it can be ordered online. You may or may not be able to prove that you and your dog are *communicado* with the Bow-Lingual, but at the very least you'll be thoroughly entertained and be spending quality time with your dog.

CAN DOGS REALLY TALK?

Dr. Doolittle talked to the animals and so does Cindy Huff of Animal Communication, Massage, and Healing Touch. She's been communicating with animals professionally for two years but discovered her ability to communicate with animals as a child. She "talks" mostly to dogs, predominantly basset hounds and greyhounds through rescue organizations such as Guardian Angel Basset Rescue and Greyhound Pets of America. Her own bassets, Beau and Maggie Mae, are rescue dogs. "I also talk with a good number of horses." She adds, "I seem to be talking with more cats these days." She says she's even talked to dogs that have recently passed over.

Huff says, "I look at myself as a bridge builder and teacher, someone who bridges a language gap between animals and their humans, someone who also teaches humans basic communication techniques with the animals they love." In the case of rescued dogs, where the animal's history is unknown and there are often health or behavior issues, being able to communicate with one's pet becomes especially valuable.

KINDRED SPIRITS

"I've grown up with animals my entire life and was very close to all of them," says Animal Communicator Mary Argo, who works mostly with domestic animals but has also talked to goats, llamas, turtles, and even a crab. "I knew when things were wrong with the animals, but I assumed everyone could pick up on these feelings." She says it all came together for her when she read a book called *Kinship with All Life* written in the 1950s by J. Allen Boone. "That book changed my life," Argo says. "I decided from then on that was what I wanted to do."

Argo says she deals with a wide variety of issues or problems, which might range from litter box issues for cats to conflicts among animals in a household. "Many consultations are about how the animal is feeling physically," Argo says. "I make it very clear that I am NOT a vet and I cannot diagnose, but I can help the person understand how the animal is feeling and perhaps refer them to a vet who might be able to help the animal."

DIRECT-DIAL DIALOGUE

Both of the animal communicators interviewed said they ordinarily conduct their work over the telephone, using a photo or the owner's detailed physical description of the animal and then making a "heart connection" with it. Some communicators even work via e-mail, so again there is no body language or any physical reference to work from, but the results are still amazingly accurate, astounding even skeptics. So how does it work?

Huff explains, "I receive emotions, pictures, physical sensations in my body (especially when asking them how they are feeling in their body), sounds, tastes, words, fleeting nuances. It depends very much on the animal."

Both Argo and Huff said they sometimes are physically present with the animal for a session, which usually lasts anywhere from 30 to 60 minutes. At these sessions, the communicator typically picks up body language cues as well as vocalizations to augment the telepathic signals they receive from the animals. "With most dogs, I can interpret some vocalizations but not all," Argo says. "Some dogs love to hear themselves talk, and they vocalize just to hear the sound of their own voice." Bruno's owner no doubt would agree.

Both women said they prefer to be called animal communicators, not animal psychics, which people find more intimidating or off-putting because the term "psychic" implies that animal communicators are soothsayers who make predictions or have supernatural powers other people don't have. "I try to impress on my clients that anyone can talk to their animals and that it just takes practice and not special skills," says Argo. "It's very similar to learning a new language." Becoming *bow*lingual, you might say.

So, what's next, talking cats? Takara reportedly released the Meow-Lingual in Japan, but it never scratched the surface of the American market. Perhaps that's because the hardest part about communicating with your cat with the Meow-Lingual would be putting the doggoned microphone on its collar.

WHISPER IN MY EAR

If you have ever seen the movie, *The Horse Whisperer*, starring Robert Redford, you probably already have a good grasp of what a dog whisperer does. A whisperer is called in for a crisis situation and often is the owner's only hope of keeping the animal. As with horse whisperers, dog whisperers can help you to see the world through your dog's eyes and understand why he behaves the way he does. More important, you'll learn how to correct and control unwanted behaviors in your pet.

Known for his *National Geographic* TV series, *The Dog Whisperer*, Cesar Millan has been called the Dr. Phil for dogs. He says he helps the dogs then retrains their owners. Remember, there are no problem dogs, only problem people. Millan employs a "Power of the Pack" approach in his training.

The trouble is that people lavish love and attention on their dogs without first expecting them to do anything to earn it. That puts the dog in control over you. By requiring the dog to perform a task before receiving his reward, you establish your dominance as the leader of his pack. The dog will strive to please you and be happier and better adjusted. That approach has often been known to work with kids, too.

Here are some training tips based on those of the Dog Whisperer. Note that it's recommended to consult a professional in matters of training problem dogs (or people):

Tip #1 The entire family should be involved in the decision to bring a new dog home. How responsibilities are to be shared for the dog's care should be established before the dog arrives.

Tip #2 The breed of dog you choose should fit your lifestyle. If you're a couch spud, don't choose active breeds, such as hunting dogs and herding dogs, which require lots of activity and exercise. By the same token, if you're a runner, don't choose a plodding, short-legged breed, like the basset hound.

Tip #3   Maintaining the health and happiness of a dog is a responsibility. Before you commit, ask yourself if you are ready for that responsibility. Do you have the time or patience to do what is required for a dog?

Tip #4   Some dogs come with a history. When adopting an older dog, be aware that he may have had negative experiences in his former home that could affect his reactions toward people, kids, or other animals.

Tip #5   When you bring home a new dog, he expects and deserves your time and attention. Take time out daily to establish rules, set boundaries, exercise him, and then give him affection.

Tip #6   Give the dog something to accomplish before you share food, water, toys, or affection. Rewards should be earned.

Tip #7   Make time for exercising your dog daily for at least 45 minutes.

Tip #8   To show your dog who's boss, always be the first one to walk in or out of a door. Don't let him barge ahead of you.

Tip #9   It can be a drag being dragged down the street at the end of the leash, especially if you're a human. Your dog should follow the leader—YOU! Don't let your dog lead you when walking him. Keep him beside you or behind you. That way he knows who's leading whom.

Tip #10 Owning a dog costs money—sometimes a lot of money if a medical emergency arises. Put aside some cash in your doggy bank and budget for your dog's care, training, and other expenses. Consider purchasing pet insurance to help with veterinary bills. Most vets demand payment at the time services are rendered.

The number of households in the United States with a dog is at 43.5 million and rising. We may not yet have gone entirely to the dogs, but there's no denying we live more and more in a dog-meet-dog society. Learning to better understand your dog can only serve to enhance your relationship with him. Whether you do that through an animal communicator, a techie translator, or a dog whisperer, take time to get in touch with your inner dog. Your best friend will thank you in ways no human ever could.

PART 4

DOG HEALTH

CHAPTER 11

Basic Dog Health

Y ou love your dog, so of course you want him to be healthy—
alert, bright-eyed, with a lustrous coat and sweet breath.
It's no fun for you or your dog if he suffers with constant
itching, hair loss, vomiting or diarrhea, or stinky dog breath. Believe it or not, it doesn't take repeated visits to the veterinarian or
costly drugs to have a healthy dog. All it takes is common sense
and vigilance. All it takes is regular preventive care.

What does *preventive care* mean? It means taking care of your
dog the way you take care of yourself. It means:

- 🐾 Brushing him regularly.
- 🐾 Checking his eyes, ears, and mouth regularly.
- 🐾 Keeping his toenails short.
- 🐾 Feeding him a high-quality food.
- 🐾 Making sure he always has access to cool, clean water.
- 🐾 Keeping his environment clean.
- 🐾 Giving him the attention and exercise he needs.
- 🐾 Spaying or neutering your dog.
- 🐾 Keeping him current on all his vaccines.
- 🐾 Taking him for a regular veterinary checkup at least once
  a year.

Preventive care means you're in touch with your dog's physical and mental condition. Let's look at each of the areas of preventive care mentioned above and see how they benefit you and your dog.

REGULAR BRUSHING

Regular brushing accomplishes so many things! First, it removes dead hair and stimulates new hair growth. It invigorates the skin and coat, adding shine while removing any knots that may be forming and any dirt or dead skin that's sitting in the coat. Brushing feels good to your dog, and he will look forward to having his coat brushed gently and thoroughly. Because your dog will enjoy being brushed regularly, you'll enjoy brushing him. Grooming sessions are great bonding sessions! But even more important, they're your opportunity to check your dog's skin and coat for any problems.

Did you know the skin is the largest organ in the body? We'll talk more about common skin problems later in this chapter, but for now, it's enough to say that because it's the largest organ, it's the most exposed part of the body, and is therefore subject to the greatest onslaught of environmental elements. Your dog's skin and coat are prime targets for ticks, fleas, prickly seed pods, sharp objects such as barbed wire or splinters, all sorts of allergens, and the hosts of bacteria that are everywhere.

By brushing your dog regularly, you'll be able to spot fleas or the tell-tale sign of their presence, "flea dirt," which is the digested blood fleas excrete after a meal. Flea dirt looks like little flecks of pepper sprinkled on your dog's skin. If you wet a paper towel and rub the "dirt" with it, you'll find it dissolves to a rusty red color—blood. If you see flea dirt on your dog, the fleas are not far away, and you'll need to take immediate action to rid your dog and your home of the problem. (Learn how to deal with fleas later in this chapter.)

Brushing will also expose any ticks that may have gotten onto your dog. There are all different kinds and sizes of ticks, carrying various diseases. Of course, you must remove any tick you find on your dog right away (learn how later in this section), but the sooner you find it, the less likely it is that there will be an infection. You'll also notice cuts, scrapes, and patches of red, swollen, or hairless skin if you brush your dog regularly. Again, the sooner you find them, the sooner you can treat and relieve them.

CHECKING EYES, EARS, AND MOUTH

Eyes

It doesn't take a lot of work to check your dog's eyes—after all, if you're like me, you spend so much time looking into them already that it's no big deal. But to keep your dog's eyes free from infection, you need to see beyond his best-begging look or his I-love-you-madly look and notice whether there's a buildup of secretion in the corners of his eyes, or any swelling or redness around the eye. It's even possible for your dog to scratch his cornea on sharp grass. To remove secretory buildup around the eyes, use gentle materials such as tissues or a soft towel and cleansers specially formulated for use around the eye. Soap stings dogs' eyes, too! If you notice redness, swelling, or scratches, a trip to the veterinarian is warranted.

Ears

Does your dog have floppy ears or erect ears—long, hairy ears or cropped ears? If you have a prick-eared or cropped-eared dog, you will have to worry less about dirty ears that can lead to infected ears, because more air gets into the inner surfaces of the ear flaps. If your dog has floppy ears, no matter the length or thickness of fur on them, you'll need to make sure you check the inner surfaces frequently. The warm, moist environment under the dog's ear is the perfect host to dirt and bacteria buildup. Proper ear-cleaning procedures are described in Part 2, in the Grooming chapter. Study them and make a point of looking under your dog's ears every few days.

Mouth

Isn't doggy breath the worst? Make sure your family never has to suffer from it by taking proper care of your dog's teeth and mouth. Dogs form plaque and tartar just as we do, but until we can teach them how to use a toothbrush, they need our help to keep their pearly-whites spick-and-span. Don't despair—it's easy to do. There are all sorts of brushes and doggy toothpastes available, or you can use a moist scrap of cheesecloth sprinkled with baking soda and get the same results. Don't use human toothpaste on your dog! What you want to do is just run a toothbrush or the cheesecloth over your dog's teeth near the gum line so you loosen the particles. No need to rinse—your dog will do that when he drinks some water.

Another reason you want to check your dog's mouth regularly is to spot problems such as chipped teeth, swollen gums, or any cuts. If you notice any of these, call your veterinarian.

TOENAILS

Keep those toenails short! Overgrown toenails can cause your dog's feet to splay, can lead to bone and joint problems, and can even grow so long that they curl under the foot and into the foot pads. Not good! There are a variety of doggy nail clippers you can use. Experiment to see which you're most comfortable with. (How to clip nails is explained in detail in Part 2, in the Grooming chapter.)

Cool, Clean Water

Would you want to drink the lukewarm, slobbery water left in the bottoms of people's water glasses after a meal? No way! Well, your dog doesn't know enough not to drink the canine equivalent that's often left in his bowl, and because he needs to drink to stay hydrated, he'll drink it anyway. So if you only fill the water bowl once a day or when you get around to it, don't be surprised if your dog gets an upset stomach or diarrhea occasionally. He needs fresh water all day long. Change the water in his bowl several times a day, and make sure to wash the bowl.

Environment

When was the last time you washed your dog's bed? How about picking up after your dog in the yard—do you do it regularly? If you don't keep your dog's environment clean, it will affect not only him, but your whole family. You don't want your dog tracking feces in on his paws when he comes in from the yard, and you don't want a smelly, dirty dog bed in the middle of your family room. So keep your dog's environment clean and you'll all feel better for it.

Attention and Exercise

If you don't provide enough of these, you'll be spending a lot of time trying to solve common behavior problems. It's a fact: Dogs are social animals. Hey, we domesticated them, so it's our own fault that they want to be with us all the time—that they're happiest when we're with them, stroking their heads or curling up on the couch together. But don't forget they're animals, and even a toy breed needs to have his body and mind exercised. Take your dog for a walk. Play ball with him in the backyard. Teach him some tricks. Make sure he minds his manners. All these things keep his mind and body active—two key elements of health.

SPAYING OR NEUTERING YOUR DOG

Consider spaying your female or neutering your dog as preventive care for a number of reasons. Healthwise, a spayed female is far less prone to diseases of the reproductive system, because she does not have a uterus, fallopian tubes, or ovaries. A neutered male, one without testicles, is immune to testicular and prostate cancers. As for behavior, you'll be spared the mess of the female's biannual "season," and your male will be less likely to lift his leg in your home, roam in search of females in heat, or engage in aggressive behavior.

VACCINES AND YOUR VETERINARIAN

From the time your dog was a wee pup he received vaccinations to protect him from major infectious diseases such as distemper, parvovirus, leptospirosis, hepatitis, and of course, rabies. Don't desert him now! Your dog needs his vaccines updated regularly, and there's no excuse for missing them. Your veterinarian will make sure you know when your dog's due, so make the appointment and take your dog in for his shots. The organisms responsible for some of these diseases can also infect people, so the health of your dog and your family is at stake.

Your veterinarian will want to see your dog at least once a year—not just to make sure he's up on his shots, but to give his professional opinion on the overall health of your dog. The vet will examine your dog from head to tail, including his eyes, ears, mouth, feet, limbs, chest, back, and anus. He will ask you about any lumps or bumps he might detect, or any swellings or tender spots. He'll let you know if your dog's teeth need a scraping (as ours do occasionally), and he'll advise you about your dog's weight and overall condition. If you've been following the preventive measures described here, you will be proud to hear your veterinarian tell you how healthy your dog looks and acts. Way to go! That's a compliment to the kind of care you're giving your best friend. Keep it up.

BASIC CARE FOR YOUR DOG

Let's face it—even with the best preventive care, things are going to happen to your dog. He's going to get fleas, he'll cut himself, he may develop a cough. He'll start limping or scratching or throwing up. Then what are you going to do? Don't despair—we're going to cover all of the following:

- 🐾 Vaccines and what they protect against.
- 🐾 Combating and controlling ticks and fleas.
- 🐾 What to do about worms.
- 🐾 First aid and emergencies.
- 🐾 Common problems of the skin, eyes, ears, mouth, nose, digestive system, respiratory system, circulatory system, nervous system, musculoskeletal system, urinary system, and reproductive system.

VACCINES AND WHAT THEY PROTECT AGAINST

A vaccine is intended to work with the immune system to fight against invasive infections of bacteria and viruses. The injection contains a harmless amount of the organism the body may someday need to fight off. This "jump-starts" the immune system to respond to that organism again if it enters the body. Without vaccines, dogs are far more susceptible to contracting infectious diseases from other dogs and other animals.

Veterinarians typically begin a vaccination schedule for a puppy at about six weeks of age. At this time the pup receives a shot for distemper and measles. Approximately eight weeks later, at fourteen to sixteen weeks of age, the pup needs his DHLPP shot, a combination vaccine for distemper, hepatitis, leptospirosis, parainfluenza virus, and parvovirus. The veterinarian may also vaccinate the pup against rabies at this time. Expect to take your dog in for his DHLPP shot every year thereafter, and for his rabies shot as necessary, depending on which vaccine your veterinarian uses (some need to be boostered more often than others). In some parts of the country, veterinarians recommend that dogs receive a vaccine for the tick-borne Lyme disease, too.

DISTEMPER

This is a viral disease that attacks a dog's gastrointestinal (digestive), respiratory, and nervous systems. It can strike at any age, but is most deadly if acquired young, which is why it's one of the first shots a pup receives. A dog with distemper will secrete a thick, yellowish discharge from his nose and eyes. He'll run a fever and he will not want to eat. The pneumonia, encephalitis, and dehydration that can result can be deadly.

INFECTIOUS CANINE HEPATITIS

Another viral disease, hepatitis attacks body tissue, particularly the liver, and most often strikes dogs under twelve months of age.

Symptoms are mild and include increased thirst, loss of appetite, abdominal discomfort, and lack of energy. Death is sudden and there is no specific treatment.

CANINE LEPTOSPIROSIS

Lepto strikes the liver and also the kidneys, but this disease is caused by bacteria. Severe infections cause shock and death, but if it's caught early, aggressive treatment with antibiotics can fight it off. Symptoms include vomiting, excessive thirst with decreased urination and dehydration, and abdominal pain. Lepto is highly contagious, and an infected dog can also pass the bacteria through his urine for some time, even after treatment. The disease is also contagious to people.

PARAINFLUENZA VIRUS

Parainfluenza is one of the germs involved in what's commonly called "kennel cough," a respiratory condition that results in a harsh, dry cough. Kennel cough is highly contagious and is so named because it is usually acquired where many dogs live together, such as in a kennel. Kennel cough can be treated with antibiotics, rest, and the proper environment. Affected dogs must be isolated from other dogs, and especially from puppies, who are more severely stricken than older dogs.

PARVOVIRUS

This viral infection manifests itself as an inflammation of the intestinal lining, causing sudden vomiting, bloody diarrhea, a high fever, and rapid weight loss. It is transmitted through the feces and can survive outside a dog's body for three to six months. The disease is extremely debilitating and rapidly lethal; treatment is intensive and often unsuccessful.

Rabies

The rabies virus attacks the central nervous system, causing unpredictable and often aggressive behavior. This erratic behavior is what, in turn, can cause the virus to spread, because it is through the bite of an infected animal that another animal is infected. Rabies can be transmitted from species to species, too, making it a health hazard to domesticated animals and people. This is why all states require that dogs and cats be vaccinated against rabies. Rabies is common in the northeastern United States, where there are large populations of skunks, raccoons, foxes, bats, and groundhogs. If you observe erratic behavior in any of these animals, call your local animal warden immediately.

Lyme Disease

Lyme disease is a tick-borne viral disease that causes often-debilitating joint pain. Although a vaccine exists to protect against Lyme, check with your veterinarian for his or her opinion about whether your dog would really benefit.

Combating and Controlling Fleas

Fleas have been annoying humankind and animals for centuries, and they're almost as tough to control today as they were in the days of ancient Rome. The flea's exoskeleton is amazingly resilient, and fleas can jump several hundred feet to land on an unsuspecting host.

The Flea Life Cycle

Despite what many dog owners believe, fleas do not spend most of their lives on their pets. In fact, fleas only stay on dogs to feed and breed. They feed by biting the dog and sucking its blood. Because fleas often harbor tapeworm larvae in their systems, fleas can transmit tapeworm disease to the animal through the bloodstream or by being eaten when a dog tries to chew the fleas off himself. When fleas mate, the females lay hundreds of eggs. These drop off the dog and into the environment. Larvae hatch from the eggs in two to three weeks, and these feed on environmental debris such as human or animal dandruff, mold, and other protein and vegetable matter. From the larval stage, the flea develops a cocoon shell in which it matures. In the cocoon stage, the flea can live with no nutrients for almost a year. Then all it takes is the slight vibration of an animal's passing for the cocoon to release the adult, which jumps onto its host and begins the life cycle all over again.

Does Your Dog Have Fleas?

Your dog can pick up fleas almost anywhere—outdoors, in a neighbor's house, even from another dog. Chances are, by the time you spot adult fleas on your dog, you have an infestation in your home and/or yard.

You'll know you and your dog are in trouble when you see him itching or licking himself suddenly and with real purpose. To confirm your suspicions, part your dog's hair to the skin or brush it backwards and see if you notice any black specks. The specks can be dense around the dog's groin area, in the hair at the base of the tail, and around the ears and neck. With a moist paper towel, wipe the specks. If they turn red, they're flea dirt—particles of digested blood the flea has excreted.

What to Do?

Now that you know your dog has fleas, you will have to be diligent about removing them from the dog *and* the environment. If you only remove the fleas from your dog without eliminating the flea eggs, larvae, and cocoons from the environment, you are guaranteed a continuing problem.

Dog owners are fortunate to have a wide range of flea-fighting products to choose from, ones that are safer than ever for dogs and the environment. You should consult with your veterinarian before waging a war on the fleas that have infiltrated your happy home; you'll want to be sure that the products you select for use on your dog and your home are appropriate for your dog's age, weight, and skin type, and that the ingredients don't clash with a product you choose for your home and yard.

The active ingredient in many of the topical flea products on the market these days is pyrethrin, a natural compound that's toxic to fleas but won't harm pets or people. There are also formulations that stop flea eggs from developing, interrupt the reproductive cycle, and break down the flea's tough exoskeleton.

Once you've selected the flea-fighters you'll need, plan a systematic approach to ridding your dog, home, and yard of all stages of the flea life cycle. Take every step seriously if you want to completely eliminate the problem. You'll need to vacuum thoroughly, using several vacuum-cleaner bags and disposing of them all in airtight plastic bags. You'll need to wash all the dog's bedding in very hot water. This may include your family's bedding, too, if the dog shares anyone's bed. Any place that your dog passes through or sleeps in can be considered a flea "hot spot" and potentially infested. Concentrate your efforts here.

To remove fleas on your dog, wash with a flea-killing shampoo, then comb thoroughly with a fine-toothed flea comb. Dip the comb in a large glass of soapy water to drown any fleas that survived the bath. Dry your dog thoroughly, and don't let him roll in his favorite hole in the yard or lie down in his usual spot on the porch—these are possible hot spots, too, and need to be treated with an outdoor insecticide.

Once you've treated the dog, house, and yard, you'll never want to repeat the process, so you'll need to step up your preventive measures.

Preventing a Flea Problem

Figuring your dog can get fleas any time he steps out of your home and into a well-populated area, you should check him regularly before coming inside. Run a flea comb through his fur. This will snag any freeloaders before they start breeding. Kill them on the comb by crushing them with your fingernail or immersing the comb in a glass of soapy water. During the warm months, when fleas are at their worst, bathe your dog regularly with a flea-preventive shampoo, and ask your veterinarian about other products designed to keep fleas from settling on your pet. Vacuum your home frequently, and make sure to keep your pet's bedding fresh and clean.

Flea Bite Sensitivity

Many dogs are allergic to the saliva that fleas inject into their skin when they bite them, or are particularly sensitive to fleas living on them. These dogs can develop serious skin ailments from their allergies and sensitivities, which often linger even after the flea problem has been eradicated. The excessive scratching, licking, and fur-biting they indulge in to get at the fleas leaves their skin damaged, causing further itching and, often, infection. The infection can leave the skin swollen or patchy and can lead to permanent hair loss. Besides being unsightly, a flea allergy or sensitivity is extremely irritating to your dog. Your veterinarian will advise you on how best to treat this many-symptomed problem.

COMBATING AND CONTROLLING TICKS

There are many types of ticks throughout the United States, the most common being the brown tick, the wood tick, and the deer tick. All adult ticks seek out dogs and other animals as hosts for feeding and breeding. The brown tick is typically the size of a match head or small pea when engorged. The wood tick is a larger tick that, when full, swells to the size of a kernel of corn. The deer tick is a tiny tick that even when engorged is no larger than a speck. The brown tick is known to transmit Rocky Mountain spotted fever, while the deer tick is the carrier of Lyme disease, both of which can be deadly.

Ridding Your Dog of Ticks

The sooner you spot a tick or ticks on your dog, the better. You need to remove the tick(s) immediately, then monitor the spot from which you removed it. To take a tick off your dog, first wet a cotton ball with alcohol or a dab of petroleum jelly. Apply this to the tick to suffocate or numb it. Then, with tweezers or with gloves on your hands, pull the tick gently off the dog. Deposit the tick in a jar filled with alcohol or nail polish remover. If your dog comes out of a trip to the woods loaded with ticks, you may want to get a tick dip from your veterinarian to help remove them all at once.

Tick bites rarely become infected, but you'll want to keep an eye on your dog's skin in the area from which the tick was pulled off, especially if it was a deer tick. Often a red, circular rash will develop around the bite—an early indicator of Lyme disease. If you notice any redness or swelling in the area of a tick bite, make an appointment to have it checked by the veterinarian.

Long-Lasting Help?

Unfortunately, it's almost impossible to keep ticks off your dogs if you spend any time outdoors with them. Your best bet, yet again, is preventive care: bathing your dog with a flea and tick shampoo formulated for his needs, taking your veterinarian's advice about what products work best to keep ticks off your dog, and always checking your dog thoroughly when you return from an outdoors adventure.

WHAT TO DO ABOUT WORMS

Like the infectious diseases that are easily avoided by proper vaccinations, worms (intestinal parasites) are another potentially deadly enemy of your dog's health that are easily avoided by proper care, hygiene, and attention.

There are several types of worms that infect dogs. Tapeworms, whipworms, roundworms, hookworms, and heartworms are the most common.

Dogs become infected by worms by contact with contaminated soil; raw, contaminated meat (such as a dead animal in the woods); or ingestion of an infected host (such as a flea). That's why it's so important to clean up after your dog in the yard and around the house, and to have fecal exams performed by the veterinarian regularly (microscopic examination is often the only way to detect the presence of internal parasites).

Treating Worms

You might suspect your puppy or dog has worms if his appetite decreases, he has an upset stomach, he loses weight, and you see blood or mucus in his stools. These symptoms are characteristic of an advanced state of parasitic infection; dogs can have a slight infection and appear normal until your veterinarian detects worms in his feces. For common infestations, safe, effective, and fast-acting worming medications are available.

Heartworm

The heartworm is a particularly deadly parasite because it infests and grows in the canine heart. Left untreated, heartworms literally strangle the heart, causing it to fail and the dog to die.

Heartworm is transmitted by infected mosquitoes. When they land on a dog to bite, heartworm larvae are deposited on the skin. The larvae burrow their way through the dog's skin, growing into small worms as they go. When they finally reach a blood vein, the worms travel to the heart, where they mature. Heartworms can grow 4 to 12 inches long, and a dog can be infected for years before symptoms are noticeable. A dog diagnosed with heartworm is in trouble either way. Treatment is intense and can even cause the death it seeks to avoid.

Today's dog owners are extremely fortunate to have heartworm preventive medication readily available. In some parts of the country veterinarians suggest giving dogs the preventive daily or monthly (depending on the type) only in seasons in which the mosquito is most active; in other parts of the country, veterinarians keep dogs on the preventive all year round as a safety precaution. Ask your veterinarian what's best for your dog and stick with the program. If you take your dog off preventive for more than several months, he must be tested for the presence of heartworm before being allowed to go back on it.

CHAPTER 12

Common Health Problems

THE SKIN

The dog's skin is a dynamic and vital organ. No matter if your dog is short- or longhaired, his skin is always shedding dead cells and replacing them with new ones. The skin is made of two layers: the epidermis, or outer layer of skin cells, and the dermis, or second layer. A dog's skin is prone to many problems that can affect either or both layers of skin—most notably, itching, hair loss, swelling and inflammation, and flaking. Because skin problems are often the most visible and pronounced of ailments afflicting dogs, it's not surprising that they represent a large percentage of the overall cases referred to veterinarians.

Scratching and Itching

While all animals occasionally scratch themselves (including us humans!), excessive or constant scratching or itching is the sign of a problem. The most common causes are fleas, hypersensitivity (an immunologic or allergic reaction), and pyoderma (a bacterial infection). If the underlying cause isn't determined, the condition can grow worse.

At the first signs of itching, check your dog for fleas. As described earlier in this chapter, you can do this by moving the fur backwards and looking for fleas themselves, or for "flea dirt"—the digested blood fleas excrete that indicates their presence. If your dog has fleas, you will need to remove them from his body and from the environment.

Some dogs are so sensitive to flea bites that they develop flea allergy dermatitis. The dog develops an immunologic hypersensitive reaction to the saliva injected by the flea when it feeds on the dog. By constantly licking, scratching, and chewing at his skin, the dog develops areas of hair loss, which can further progress to open sores that lead to infection. The area most affected seems to be the base of the tail and lower back.

Flea allergy dermatitis typically develops when a dog is three to five years old, and it can be extremely tough to reverse, even if your dog is flea-free! The sooner your veterinarian can diagnose the condition, the sooner you can begin treatment and hope to alleviate the symptoms. Treatment will involve being vigilant about keeping your dog and home flea-free, the use of special shampoos, dips, or ointments to prevent itching, and possibly a prescription for anti-inflammatory drugs.

Dogs can also develop immunologic hypersensitivities to foods—anything from beef to wheat to dairy. This is why so many premium diets feature ingredients such as lamb, rice, or turkey.

Allergies

A hypersensitivity reaction to things in the environment, such as certain fabrics, detergents, molds, or fungi, usually means the dog is allergic to that thing. Symptoms usually develop when the dog is one to three years old and begin to show in the spring or fall. Areas of the body most affected include the face, stomach, paws, and, oddly enough, the creases of the elbows. If your dog is constantly rubbing his face, licking and scratching his paws, or itching his tummy or elbows, you should suspect an allergic hypersensitivity. Left untreated, the itching will lead to areas of broken, exposed skin that are ripe for infections. Often, paw licking will develop into a behavioral habit, perpetuating the condition.

Because of the enormous number of potential allergens in the dog's environment, your veterinarian will need to evaluate your dog's symptoms carefully and perform blood and skin tests to try to determine the allergen. Once this is pinpointed, elimination of the source is necessary, and you will probably need to use special shampoos and ointments to alleviate itching.

Infections

Bacterial infection is the result of skin that's under attack and losing the battle. The skin of a healthy dog has certain bacteria that live on its surface and within the hair's follicles. This "good" bacteria wards off infection by "bad" bacteria. But when something happens to disrupt the balance, harmful bacteria invade and proliferate, causing serious infection and some severe and very painful problems.

Hot Spots

These are quarter-sized areas of red, moist, swollen sores, typically found on longhaired dogs during warm, humid weather. They can be caused by the dog's licking itself in response to some other problem such as a parasitic infection, or general hypersensitivity.

Often the cause goes undiscovered. Treatment involves applying antibiotic ointment to the wound and using an Elizabethan collar on the dog so he cannot reach the spot to continue licking or chewing at it.

Skin-Fold Pyoderma

Dogs with areas of thick folded skin on their bodies, such as Chinese shar-pei, bloodhounds, mastiffs, pugs, and others, can develop infections in between the folds. That's because the fold creates a warm, moist spot—prime breeding grounds for bacteria. Regular inspection of the folds can help prevent infection, and antibiotic ointment can help treat it.

Another spot bacteria may breed rapidly is between the toes, and this is only exacerbated by the dog's licking. Scratches or cuts to the skin between the toes often go unnoticed, which can also lead to infection. Again, good grooming habits can go a long way toward preventing this condition.

Seborrhea

When there is an imbalance of new cell growth to replace dying cells, the result is a thickening of the skin with noticeable shedding of the dead cells. This is called seborrhea. Symptoms include extreme flakiness, an overall greasiness to the skin and coat, an unpleasant and persistent odor to the coat, itchiness, and bald patches of thick skin. The causes of seborrhea include hormonal imbalance, parasitic infection, excessive bathing or grooming, and nutritional disorders—all factors that contribute to the skin's not being able to properly regulate itself. Diagnosis is fairly simple, but treatment can be quite involved and may necessitate antibiotics, special shampoos, and anti-inflammatories.

COMMON PROBLEMS OF THE EYES, EARS, AND MOUTH

Eyes

Eyes and their surrounding tissues are susceptible to a number of problems. Dogs have three eyelids: top and bottom, and a third eyelid called the nictitating membrane, an extra layer of protection against the elements. The eyelids and the nictitating membrane all produce tears to lubricate the eye.

If one or both of your dog's eyes is tearing excessively, suspect a problem. It could be that a speck of dust or dirt or a grass seed has lodged between the eyelid and the eyeball. If you can see the particle, you can try to remove it with blunt tweezers or a moistened paper towel or cotton ball. To help the eye heal, apply some antibiotic ophthalmic ointment such as Neosporin just inside the lower lid.

Likewise, if an eye appears red or swollen, the dog may have an infection caused by a foreign body. It is best to consult your veterinarian if such a condition exists.

Entropion and Ectropion

Sometimes eye irritation is caused by the eyelashes rubbing against the eye. If the eyelid rolls inward, causing the eyelashes to aggravate the eye, the condition is called entropion. When the eyelid rolls outward the condition is known as ectropion. Dogs with ectropion have exposed eyelid tissue that's particularly prone to damage and infection. Entropion and ectropion are both common congenital defects that require surgical repair.

Conjunctivitis

The membrane that lines the inner sides of the eyeball up to the cornea is called the conjunctiva. If it becomes infected, you'll notice a discharge from the corner of the dog's eye. The discharge may be clear and watery or opaque and thick. Typically this is the result of a bacterial infection. Your veterinarian can give you the best diagnosis.

Eye Problems of Older Dogs

As your dog ages, he becomes prone to dry eye and cataracts. As the name implies, dry eye is a condition in which the surface of the eye appears dull instead of shiny and bright. Dry eye is a condition of the tear glands, indicating that something is at fault with them. Consequently, they cannot supply the moisture necessary to lubricate the eye properly, which in turn leads to infection. Your veterinarian may be able to stimulate the tearing mechanism, or artificial tears will be prescribed.

Cataracts are clouding of the cornea that lead to blindness. They usually appear as milky colored or bluish-gray spots in the dog's eye. All older dogs are prone to developing cataracts. Other dogs at risk are diabetic dogs and dogs with a congenital problem that causes cataracts to form early.

Ears

Dogs' ears come in all shapes and sizes, from small and erect to long and pendulous. The most common problems they're susceptible to are cuts, hematomas, and infections. Many breeds' ears are cropped both to enhance appearance and to reduce the incidence of ear infection.

The Inner Ear

The skin of a healthy inner ear should be pink with some waxy light-brown secretion in the ear canal. If you notice your dog scratching at his ears, excessively rubbing the side of his face against the floor or other surfaces, or whining with discomfort when you stroke around his ears, suspect an infection or other problem. The skin that lines the ear canal is the perfect host for bacteria, which thrive in warm, moist environments. Dogs who swim regularly, who live in humid environments, who have long, hairy ears, or whose ears are not regularly inspected for excessive dirty wax buildup can easily develop an infection. Your veterinarian will diagnose it and give you instructions for treatment.

Ear mites can be another source of itchy, inflamed inner ears. These microscopic parasites also like warm, moist environments, where they feed on skin flakes. A scraping at the vet's office will confirm this diagnosis.

The Outer Ear

Ear flaps are most prone to cuts, bites, and hematomas. As long as a cut is not deep, it is simple to treat by cleaning it thoroughly and applying antibiotic ointment. Often dogs involved in a fight will get their ears bitten. If the bite is deep, take the dog to the veterinarian; otherwise, wash it thoroughly, apply antibiotic ointment, and monitor it for infection.

Hematomas are the result of a pooling of blood in the ear flap. This can happen after a dog shakes his ears violently, scratches them excessively, or knocks them against a sharp object. Consult your veterinarian about the best way to deal with a hematoma.

Deafness

Some breeds of dogs have genetic defects that cause them to either be born deaf or develop deafness at an early age. Conscientious breeders will test their dogs if they suspect a problem and remove affected dogs from their breeding programs. This is most common in dalmatians and some terriers. Older dogs of ten lose some or all of their hearing. They still manage to get around in familiar, safe environments, but special care should be given to them.

Nose

First of all, forget the folk remedy that says a dog with a warm, dry nose is sick. Yes, a dog's nose should typically be cool and moist, and if it's not, the dog may have a fever. But some sick dogs will have cool, runny noses. Regardless, the nose is an all-important organ to the dog. Smell is his most acute sense; through it he learns the most about his environment and the other creatures in it.

Runny Nose

Because the nose itself doesn't have any sweat glands, when a dog is excited or sick, the nasal mucous membrane will secrete water. Only secretions that persist for several hours indicate a problem.

Sneezing

This indicates an irritation to the front of the nasal cavity (coughing or gagging means the irritation is further back). It could be the inhalation of dust or dirt, which would cause the dog to sneeze several times and then stop, or it could indicate a fever or infection if it persists. If the sneezing is accompanied by discharge from the nose and/or eyes, see your veterinarian.

Mouth

The dog's mouth is made up of the lips, teeth, gums, and tongue. It is the passageway to the esophagus. While the lips and tongue can be injured by cuts or burns, injury and disease most commonly affects the teeth and gums, and it is on these that we will concentrate.

Teeth

The average adult dog has forty-two teeth in his mouth (this can vary by breed, with shorter-faced breeds having less teeth). With improper oral hygiene, the teeth can become encrusted with plaque and tartar, leading to smelly (dog) breath, inflamed or infected gums, tooth loss, and general deterioration of the mouth.

Because of the high incidence of dogs suffering from periodontal disease, veterinarians and others in the pet industry have gone out of their way to educate owners and provide them with materials that make taking care of their dogs' teeth easy.

Healthy puppies and young dogs have bright white teeth and pink gums. It is possible to keep your dog's teeth looking almost as good as they did when he was a pup. This requires regular brushing, proper feeding and chew toys, and inspection for problems.

Get your dog used to having his mouth handled by regularly lifting his lips and gently opening his mouth. Look at his teeth and gums. Is the gum line red or swollen? Are the teeth white all the way to the gums? Do you see any chipped teeth?

You should brush your dog's teeth several times a week. To do this, you can purchase one of several types of doggy toothbrushes on the market. Some even come with their own doggy toothpaste that's specially flavored so dogs like the taste. Remember, never use human toothpaste on your dog. He won't like it, and it's bad for him. If you don't want to try the special toothbrushes and paste, you can wrap a small strip of gauze or cheesecloth around your finger to use as a scrubber. Use a paste of baking soda and water as the dentrifice. To brush, lift your dog's lip and brush or rub against the teeth with your finger. Try to get the brush or your finger all the way to the back of the mouth to reach the molars. Open the mouth and move the brush or your finger along the inside of the teeth along the gum line. Work quickly, gently, and thoroughly. The whole process should only take a few minutes. When you're finished, reward your dog with a crunchy snack— dogs love those miniature carrots!

During your annual checkups at the veterinarian's office, the doctor can advise you whether your dog's teeth need to be surgically scraped to have any lingering or stubborn tartar removed. Since this procedure requires anesthesia, discuss it with your vet at length before subjecting your dog to it.

Gums

Healthy gums are pink and should be firm. Red, swollen, painful gums are a sign of gingivitis and require immediate attention. Your veterinarian will probably need to scrape your dog's teeth to remove offending tartar, after which you'll need to aggressively brush and inspect your dog's teeth. Severe gingivitis can lead to infection and tooth decay.

Choking and Gagging

If your dog starts to choke or gag, there may be something caught in the back of his mouth. If possible, try to remove the object yourself. If it's lodged too firmly and your dog is struggling and choking, take him to the veterinarian immediately. Try to calm and reassure the dog.

THE DIGESTIVE SYSTEM

This system is made up of the esophagus, stomach, small intestine, liver, gall bladder, spleen, colon, rectum, and anus. The problems most typically associated with this system are:

Vomiting
Bloat
Diarrhea
Constipation
Flatulence
Anal sac disorders

Every dog will experience upsets of the digestive system in the course of his life; most problems are easily treated and symptoms resolve within hours or days.

Vomiting

If your dog is vomiting, there is definitely something wrong with him. Determining what that something is, however, is trickier than you might think. You'll need to take special note of what he vomits and how he vomits to figure out what's wrong.

The most common cause of vomiting is simply overeating, or eating so quickly the food is gulped down and then comes back up again. Dogs will also commonly vomit after eating grass, and some dogs get carsick and vomit in the car. If your dog vomits what's obviously partly digested food or chewed grass and only vomits once or twice, or is distressed by the car, don't worry about it. If you notice blood in the vomit, or if the vomiting is severe and frequent, make an appointment to see the veterinarian. These are signs that your dog is truly not well.

Bloat

This condition is also called gastric dilatation, which is exactly what it is: a swelling up of the stomach due to gas, fluid, or a combination. When the stomach fills up this way, it is prone to twisting, which quickly leads to shock and death. Dogs can develop bloat by eating too much dry kibble; exercising vigorously after eating, or gulping their food or their water. Some breeds seem prone to it, and it appears to run in some breed lines. Dogs experiencing bloat become restless, drool heavily, try to vomit or defecate unsuccessfully, and cry in pain when their stomachs are palpated. It is imperative to get your dog to the veterinarian as soon as possible if you suspect bloat.

Diarrhea

Like vomiting, the type and consistency of diarrhea vary depending on what's really wrong with the dog. When all is normal, the dog eats and drinks and his digestive system absorbs nutrients from the food and water and passes along undigested materials in the stool, which should be firm and consistent in color. Any irritation to the intestines or the bowel will trigger diarrhea. These irritations can vary from a change in food or water, to overexcitement, to eating something that can't be digested or is toxic, or that produces an allergic response. The color, consistency, odor, and frequency of the diarrhea can help you and your veterinarian determine the underlying cause and set about providing the proper treatment.

Constipation

If you notice your dog straining to defecate, or even whimpering or whining while doing so, with the result being no passing of stool, your dog is constipated. Most cases of constipation are caused by inappropriate diet, which causes stools to form improperly and either block the colon or be painful to pass. Try giving your dog one-half to two tablespoons of a gentle laxative such as milk of magnesia. Take the dog out often so you don't risk an accident in the house. If you don't get results in twelve to twenty-four hours, consult your veterinarian.

Flatulence

Having an overly flatulent dog is no fun! Through no fault of his own, a dog who passes gas can clear an entire room in no time. Peeyew! Chalk your dog's flatulence up to inappropriate diet yet again. A diet high in meats, fermentable foods such as onions, beans, or even some grains, or dairy products can lead to excess gas. Review your dog's diet carefully, including the ingredient list of his dog food, and slowly integrate a diet change. If this doesn't yield results, your veterinarian can help.

Anal Sac Disorders

Dogs have two anal sacs, one on each side of the rectum at about five and seven o'clock, commonly called "scent sacs." They secrete a distinctive odor that leaves the dog's scent when he defecates. If the sacs become blocked, they can become sore and infected and will need to be expressed. If your dog frequently scoots across the floor dragging his bottom or wants to lick the area often, suspect an anal sac problem and ask the vet to show you how to handle expressing them to relieve the buildup.

THE RESPIRATORY SYSTEM

Dogs breathe through their respiratory system, a series of airways comprised of the nasal passages, throat, windpipe, and bronchial tubes that lead to the lungs. Any of the following symptoms indicate a problem in the system:

Rapid Breathing

Dogs will breath heavily and rapidly in a number of circumstances, such as after strenuous exercise, in excessive heat, or if they're excited or stressed. If your dog is breathing rapidly while at rest and you can't attribute any of these other factors to his condition, consult your veterinarian.

Noisy Breathing

This includes wheezing, sneezing, labored breathing, hoarseness, and any odd sound the dog makes while trying to breathe. Owners of some short-faced breeds live with this problem. Their dogs have shorter airways and will regularly snort, snore, or breathe heavily. For other dogs, noisy breathing is generally due to an obstruction, though it can also indicate a lung disease or heart failure. It's best to have your veterinarian listen and look.

Coughing

Coughing results from the effort to extricate an obstruction in the airways, whether it's a bone chip, a collapsed windpipe, or a fluid buildup in the lungs caused by a respiratory disease such as kennel cough. Kennel cough is highly contagious between dogs and can spread rapidly at a dog show or in a kennel. There is a vaccine to help prevent kennel cough, and if it's caught early, treatment is successful.

THE CIRCULATORY SYSTEM

At the center of the circulatory system is the all-important heart, a muscle that pumps blood to the rest of the body. Diseases that affect the canine heart include birth defects, aging, infectious disease, and heartworms. Heartworm is a condition that can be deadly, but is easily avoided by giving regular preventive heartworm medication, as discussed earlier in this section.

THE NERVOUS SYSTEM

All activity in the nervous system generates from the brain, the spinal cord, and the peripheral nerves. Spinal cord diseases, seizures, head injuries, and paralysis are some of the problems that can result from injury or disease of this system.

Seizures and Epilepsy

A seizure is caused by a sudden burst of electrical activity in the brain, affecting the entire body by causing uncontrolled convulsions: foaming at the mouth, jerking of the limbs, snapping of the jaws, rolling of the eyes. Depending on the seizure's severity, the dog may collapse and slip into unconsciousness. Seizures can be caused by trauma to the brain or the healing associated with it, or by a hereditary condition.

Epilepsy is a state of recurrent and similar seizures that typically happen in three phases: sudden restlessness accompanied by champing or foaming at the mouth; falling to the ground with head thrown back and pupils dilated, slobbering and drooling; and a recovery phase in which the dog is disoriented. The more violent phases, one and two, happen in just a few minutes; the recovery phase may last hours. You must consult with your veterinarian and your dog's breeder if your dog has epilepsy.

Paralysis

Complete paralysis is the result of permanent damage to the spinal cord. But a dog can experience partial paralysis due to a spinal cord disease or infection. Lyme disease can reslut in paralysis with the effects of the tick bite coming on slowly, impairing movement to the point of paralysis. A speedy diagnosis is key to recovery. Normally the paralysis resolves with treatment by antibiotics.

THE MUSCULOSKELETAL SYSTEM

Bones and muscles support the body and protect the internal organs. All dogs, regardless of size, have an average of 319 different bones in their bodies. The bones are connected by ligaments and surrounded by muscles.

If your dog is limping or is favoring a particular leg (lame), chances are he's got a bone or joint disease, a strained muscle or tendon, or possibly a broken bone. The causes range from something as severe as a congenital disorder, such as hip or elbow dysplasia, to something as ordinary as a strained muscle or age-related as arthritis. Your veterinarian should give you a professional diagnosis.

Hip Dysplasia

Canine hip dysplasia (often referred to as CHD or just HD) is a disorder of the hip socket. In a healthy hip, the head of the thigh bone (femur) should fit snugly in the hip socket (acetabulum). If the ligaments around the socket are loose, the head of the femur will start to slip from the socket. This causes gradual hind-end lameness and pain. Treatment varies depending on the age of the dog, the severity of the condition, and the options available to dog and owner. Rapid advances are being made in the treatment of hip dysplasia.

While a specific cause of CHD has not been identified, it is suspected to be an inherited disorder, and breeders are encouraged to x-ray their dogs before breeding and to only breed dogs that have been certified free of the disease. It has happened, however, that CHD-free parents have produced pups that develop hip dysplasia. Weight, nutrition, and environment have all been implicated in the possible exaggeration or development of CHD, which normally manifests at an age of rapid growth.

THE URINARY SYSTEM

The components of the urinary system are the bladder, prostate, and urethra, as well as the kidneys and ureters. The system works together. The two kidneys' jobs are to siphon excess waste created by ordinary metabolism, yet regulate water and minerals. Wastes are deposited into the ureter, which empties into the bladder. Urine passes from the bladder to outside the body via the urethra (in the male, the urethra also transports semen).

If all is functioning well, your dog will urinate regularly (not frequently), and his urine will be clear and yellow in color. A problem of the kidneys, bladder, urethra, or prostate will be evident as straining to urinate, blood-tinged or cloudy urine, excessive drinking accompanied by excessive urination, or pain upon urination. The problem could be something as minor as dehydration or as complicated as renal failure. You must consult your veterinarian for a diagnosis.

THE REPRODUCTIVE SYSTEM

Of the Female

This includes two ovaries, a uterus, and fallopian tubes. A spayed female will have all of these removed. Intact females will experience regular heats and are prone to false pregnancies and infection of the uterus, called pyometra. As advised earlier in this chapter, you and your female dog will be happier and healthier if she is spayed. Some believe that a spayed bitch is prone to obesity. While it is true that she will not be under the same hormonal influence that keeps an intact bitch in form, with regular exercise and the proper diet a spayed bitch can be kept in top shape.

Of the Male

The male dog's reproductive system includes the testicles, penis, and prostate gland. Intact males are prone to damage or injury of the penis or scrotum, cancer of the testes, and inflammation, enlargement, or cancer of the prostate. Once again, you and your dog will live happier, healthier lives if the dog is neutered. Neutering is the surgical removal of the testicles. The empty scrotum eventually shrinks and leaves no scar. Neutering not only guarantees the male won't develop testicular cancer or prostate problems, it also lessens a male's territoriality, making him (with proper care and training) a friendlier pet. Neutering does not significantly change a dog's temperament, however; if you have an aggressive male, neutering will not solve the problem, but combined with training, it can certainly help.

HANDLING AN EMERGENCY

Emergencies elicit two states that don't help matters any—shock and/or fear in the dog, and panic in the owner. When dealing with an emergency, keep reminding yourself to stay calm and stay focused on what you can do for your dog. Ideally, you should have someone drive you to the clinic while you handle the dog.

After you've called the veterinary clinic, as well as someone to come help you if you're alone with the dog, follow these steps:

1. Evaluate the dog's condition and deliver any first-aid procedures, such as reducing bleeding, putting on a muzzle so the dog doesn't bite you or someone else, applying any ointment, or wrapping a wound.
2. Keep your dog still and warm by reassuring him while holding him down and keeping a blanket on him.
3. Make preparations to transport him so he experiences as little turbulence and commotion as possible.

FIND A VETERINARIAN

This is by no means a complete discussion of the health conditions that affect dogs, or their diagnosis or treatment. There are of course professional-level books far more detailed than this one. The authors suggest you consult other books for more detailed information, and most importantly, find a veterinarian you can trust and rely on. He or she will be the person you should turn to for detailed advice.

Index